CASTLEPOINT

Weather-beaten tractor at The Gap, with Castle Rock in the background leaning over the Pacific Ocean on the North Island's rugged East Coast.

CASTLEPOINT

The story of life on an iconic New Zealand
sheep and cattle station

Lorain Day

HarperCollins*Publishers*

HarperCollins*Publishers*

First published in 2011
by HarperCollins*Publishers* (New Zealand) Limited
PO Box 1, Shortland Street, Auckland 1140

HarperCollins*Publishers*
31 View Road, Glenfield, Auckland 0627, New Zealand
Level 13, 201 Elizabeth Street, Sydney, NSW 2000, Australia
A 53, Sector 57, Noida, UP, India
77–85 Fulham Palace Road, London, W6 8JB, United Kingdom
2 Bloor Street East, 20th floor, Toronto, Ontario M4W 1A8, Canada
10 East 53rd Street, New York, NY 10022, USA

National Library of New Zealand Cataloguing-in-Publication Data

Day, Lorain.
The story of life on an iconic New Zealand sheep and
cattle station / Lorain Day.
ISBN 978-1-86950-938-5
1.Castlepoint Station (N.Z.)—History. 2. Castlepoint (N.Z.)
—History. I. Title.
636.01099368—dc 22

ISBN: 978 1 86950 938 5

Project management and internal photos by Alex Hedley, unless otherwise credited
Cover and internal design by Carolyn Lewis
Front cover image by iStockphoto; back cover image by Ginny Neal; inside front cover images
by John Bougen and Alex Hedley

Printed by Bookbuilders, China

Dedicated to the memory of our sister, Kim, and with love to my husband, Brett, who is the best thing that ever happened to me.

I would also like to thank Bill Honeybone and Alex Hedley for their faith in me, and the extended family at Castlepoint Station, who welcomed me with warmth and provided me with so much wonderful material. My thanks also to Antoinette Sturny, Teresa McIntyre and the gorgeous editorial team at HarperCollins — simply the best.

Castlepoint Station

Modern-day Castlepoint Station, first settled in 1847
as one of New Zealand's first sheep runs. The station
now stretches along 12 kilometres of the Wairarapa's
coastline, covering an overall area of 2952 hectares,
made up of flat ocean terraces and imposing hill country.

CASTLEPOINT
STATION

Matai 34.64
Slack 18.04
Nans 11.39
Punga Hills 20.01
Pigroot 12.27
Erewhon-retired 7
Camp Corner 24.83
Rough Face 17.27
Erewhon 72.83
Forkes 23.71
Gungadai 14.54
Fionas 19.84
Te Hau 24.84
Toowombas
Site waste 0.3
Taven 6.47
South T
Worleys 21.08
Fleecer 8.12
Dale 6.85
Melinas 22.43
Bottor
Silts 16.34
Georginas 12.23
Junee 11.57
Bog 16.77
Hakowhai 18.99
Back Karaka 10.12
Siberia 22.0
Woolshed 5.45
Pukenui 23.71
Top
Montrose
Tamaras 17.08
Force 5.12
Bo
Back Peaks 13.75
Parkers 21.92
Front Karaka 9.57
Boundary 5.74
Rollover 19.62
Chauldons 6.16
Erdua 16.04
Valley 9.87
Drive 4.8
Boundary Lane 0.
Random Area 64.95
Big Knob 11.6
Big Knob Pines 6
Eaten Pines 5.69
Front Peaks 13.16
Kims Flat 9.63
Terumi 466.09
Triumph 6.78
Fullers 17.
Ritchies 11.82
7.93
Gardiners 16.54
Middle Creek 8.7
Saddlewood .51
Lodge Paddock 23.97

Tanaroa 18.17
Whakataki 13.24
Pleasant Valley 11.32
Pine Ridge 16.57
Mt. Kisco 16.96
Pawling 15.18
Puzzle Creek 13.67
Waikuri 12.02
Pylons 16.73
Carlsons 16.62
Waipipi 19.0
Lookout 22.53
Amawalk 9.31
Lost World 4.42
Cleavage 18.02
Sandhill 9.3
Longacre 19.18
Sunnyside 18.15
Gordons Gully 27.87
Top Roadface 16.84
Lighthouse 14.67
Plateau 30.16
Sea Face 21.31
Upper Fern 22.41
Potters 25.31
Belford 9.37
Bottom Roadface 16.06
Zig Zag 19.2
Lower Fern 34.98
Reservoir 18.96
Tabletop 13.62
Oyster Shell 34.06
Gravel Pit 27.12
2nd Rams 3.69
1st Rams 3.88
Freds Face 11.99
0.02 - 2.4
Pony 8.04
Crumps Face 13.98
Scenic 3.6
The Mound 16.07
Pony 5
North Kowhai 37.13
MacDonald Lane 0.87
Pony 1 0.9
Broken Down 14.74
Airstrip 6.97
Creek 15.56
Home Run 21.47
South Kowhai 14.02
0
Airstrip Holding 2.1
Isosceles 23.03
Williams 12.91
Stuck 15.73
Heather Hills 22.18
Netted 10.74
Willow 19.46
Greba 17.2
MacDonald 26.21
Cabbage Trees 19.63
Poplar Gully 15.48
Shed 15.64
Drayspur 24.99
Boulders 17.11
Cliffs 18.77
Toi 18.05
Bottom Castle 12.75
Chimneys 17.39
Pinch Gut 2.2
Hughes 24.98
Wheel Around 15.28
Dillys Gully 30.19
Top Castle 7.37
Switchback 23.87
West Longspur 15.18
e 18.74
Ti Tree 27.85
Misery 15.66
Muscoot 17.5
Horseshoe 13.59
Basin 41.69
Top Maruka Roa 11.25
Longspur 41.67
Burn 24.1
Wrighty 19.62
Variegated 13.53
Bottom Manuka Roa 11.74
Pukeroa 17.62
Top Centre Ground 6.72
Cob 11.57
Delta 4.01
Laing's Hill 13.06
Western Bank 11.69
Horse 16.87
Top Nagakauau 3.93
Islay 8.22
Oilslick 15.19
Murison's 22.01
Oxen 11.41
Mountain 8.71
Racecourse 9.26
Alex 5.35
Lucerne 5.58
Sandstone 22
Bullock 16.92
Short Strip 5.69
a 14.95
Loafers Flat 13.17
Bottom Nagakauau 7.09
Braewold 8.74
End of Terrace 5.87
End of Terrace Lane 4.13
Millburn 7.6
Humpy 5.83
Shags Nest 8.96
ookery Nook 7.46
Groats 5.45
N

Ewes above the Castlepoint shearing shed
at dusk, prior to the autumn shear.

Contents

The junction at Langdale Road, Whareama.

Connections

Castlepoint Station began in New Zealand in the second half of the nineteenth century, when an English farm labourer, Thomas Guthrie, arrived around the coast with a mob of sheep and cattle. At the same time, on the other side of the world, another farmer — James Wood, great-grandfather of the current owner of Castlepoint Station, Emily Crofoot — had something to say; something which was recorded in the minutes of the Bedford Farmers Club, New York State:

Mr. Wood closed the subject by saying: There is one more view of the manure question that in my opinion claims the attention of every Christian man. If I had announced that I came to talk about the 'religion of the manure heap', it would have been thought strange, at least. But you know it is said that 'we brought nothing into the world, and it is certain that we can take nothing out.' We are here to occupy and beautify this earth, which is God's footstool, and it is our duty to make it the better by having lived on it, and to leave it better for those who come after us. Now, if it were one's absolutely, and we could carry it away, this would not be true. But as it is, it should be our aim, instead of exhausting and wearing out what is committed to our use, to so employ it that we can return it to our Master in better condition, if possible, than we received it. This is a view of farming which I have never before heard advanced but which, I believe, should recommend itself to every right-thinking man.

James Wood
31 December 1869

Previous page: Farm manager at Castlepoint Station
Stu Neal, left, with shepherd Jared Roberts, homeward
bound along Castlepoint's laneway.
Ginny Neal

Disused blade shears, a relic from a bygone era at
Castlepoint Station.

Introduction

WIND. THERE'S A LOT OF IT AT CASTLEPOINT. It blows hard, and it helped shape the land and, to no small extent, the lives of the people who live there. It can be as gentle as a kitten, and as wild as a hellcat. It has blown seabirds and seals to the coast and away again, and small whales and dolphins, who are frequent visitors, know its many moods. Some days have seen the wind ease ocean-going waka and sailing ships into safe anchorage and a sheltered harbour, while others have seen similar vessels smashed against unforgiving rocks. Sometimes women and children have been able to land safely, and on other days strong men have drowned in howling gales or been caught in capricious surges. Most of the time it's a northerly of some description, ranging from the northeast to the northwest, often blowing up wild waves and heavy seas to batter the lower east coast of the North Island for days, making landfall almost impossible.

There's a nick in the coast the Pakeha settlers used to call Deliverance Cove, in deference to the haven it provided from just such relentless seas; nowadays the locals call it The Gap. Much earlier, in Maori legends that mark time in genealogies, not centuries, it provided shelter for a mischievous giant octopus from Hawaiki, who stole Kupe's bait and set him off on a long-distance pursuit which ultimately led the great Polynesian explorer to the Wairarapa coast. The octopus, or wheke, took refuge in the cavern beneath the present-day lighthouse, in a cave called Te Ana o te Wheke a Muturangi, the Cave of Muturangi's Octopus.

Much later, on 11 February 1770, English explorer Captain James Cook was making his first circumnavigation of the North Island. He sighted a huge rocky promontory prominent above the horizon, which he described that night in his journal as 'a remarkable hillock', later recording it as Castle Point on his chart.

Over time the spectacular and distinctive land formation has become known as Castle Rock, while the settlement and the station that nestled below the windswept hills and coves would become Castlepoint. From 1949 the one-word spelling became official, when the name for the area was gazetted, although cartographers continued to use Cook's original two-word version. One word or two, it doesn't matter. Say Castlepoint to any New Zealander of a certain age, and they'll know what you mean.

And what does Castlepoint mean to them, besides an iconic station, a lighthouse, a motorcamp and summer horseracing along the beach? We've seen the *Country Calendar* tributes to rugged people living it tough on a windswept coastline, raising sheep, cattle and families. Those who grew up in the 'fifties

and 'sixties will most likely have read about and been taught to admire the men and women who broke in this untamed land, a vast swath of it, turning scrub-covered hills and marshy swamp into productive farmland and helping to strengthen the economic backbone of this country. Since 1998 there have been new owners, a new family and, again, they have been migrants from the other side of the world — and for a time there were concerns about what this might mean for an iconic slice of our farming heritage. That's long since been laid to rest, and the new owners are now very much part of a small, close-knit rural community.

But there's much more to Castlepoint than this idealized image. For a start, there's the reality of a tough mistress — after all, she's no walkover, this piece of Aotearoa. Instead, there's an enduring physical environment that has absorbed the blood, sweat and tears of the many people who have lived here, through generations of Maori occupation and more than 160 years of European history. She's ready to take as much again, and more. And, as always, there are the people who made it memorable, giving her the best years of their lives. This book will share some of their stories and hopes to introduce you, albeit briefly, to the magnificence that is Castlepoint.

LORAIN DAY
AUCKLAND 2011

Opposite page:
Horse's bridle at
the stock yards.

Left: Fishing boat
tractors at The Gap,
Castlepoint.

Captain James Cook's 'remarkable hillock', Castle Rock, first sighted in 1770 during the English explorer's first circumnavigation of the North Island.

The homestead

As all country people know, the heart of any farm is the homestead. When it comes to an iconic station like Castlepoint, on the Wairarapa Coast, inevitably the homestead — and the people who live there — occupy an important place in local history. And the homestead at Castlepoint Station is a grand old lady — not because she's big, or ornate, or imposing. Quite the opposite in fact. It's more about the way she nestles comfortably into the land, weathering wild storms and ferocious 'dries' alike, a constant factor in an everchanging story.

IF YOU COME TO CASTLEPOINT STATION AT NIGHT, and from Whareama in the south, up the laneway, then you know you're going to wake up by the sea. As the road winds out of Masterton and up into the coastal hill country, you turn onto a gravel road that climbs through pine plantations in the gathering dusk. When you crest the final hill the station is spread out before you, with the unmistakable bulk of Castle Rock in the distance. While you're not on station land yet, you're close — and Castlepoint is waiting for you, defined by the line of rolling breakers and the vastness of the East Coast stretching away to the north.

On a calm morning in February, lift your eyes to the view from the kitchen table in the homestead, out through the open double doors and across the garden to the silhouette of the headland and the famous lighthouse — and you could be nowhere else in the world. Fine spray blows in from the sea as the rolling breakers sweep onto the beach, wind catching the tops of the waves and blowing them in to shore. It's even possible to make out the moving silhouettes of visitors walking on the headland, beneath the lighthouse.

There's a romance about the place, that's for sure — whether it's the initials (*JS loves GE*) carved into a flat rock below Castle Rock itself, or the story that's told of a young couple who walked up to the lighthouse, and, walking back down, found that a friend of the hopeful groom had written his marriage proposal out on the sand below; it's a place that holds many fond memories for many people.

A sealed road, Jetty Road — the main road at Castlepoint — runs along past the homestead and down to the foreshore, complete with speedbumps and streetlights, and beside the road is the letterbox for Castlepoint Station. The names on the side are A and E Crofoot: Anders and Emily, who have owned the station since 1998 when they moved here from the United States, leaving behind Braewold, a 300-acre farm in New York State that had been in Emily's family for seven generations.

Painted in crisp cream with a dark-green trim — the station colours that are slowly being incorporated from one end of the property to the other, as each of the farm's buildings and homes comes up for renovation — the solid wooden mailbox stands outside the entrance to a sweeping circular driveway, guarded by four huge Phoenix palms and banks of agapanthus. The air is ringing with the sound of cicadas, and the breeze moves gently. Today the wind is soft, but on any other day it could be an entirely different story.

The gravel driveway may be sweeping, but it's also a working driveway and usually has visitors' and farm vehicles of one kind or another parked outside,

Previous page:
The gateway to Castlepoint Station from the south at Wai Ngaio, Castle Rock looming in the distance.

Opposite page:
A late summer's morning at the 'grand old lady', Castlepoint homestead.

both at the front and the back of the house. The old weatherboard homestead is being painted again; new wood is replacing the old window facings where they have rotted out. It's slow work — scraping back, replacing the bad bits and putting on three or four coats of paint. It's the constant battle every homeowner knows, fighting the elements; but one you sense is taken seriously here, where resources are husbanded carefully and the value of things noted in non-monetary terms as well as in dollars and cents, and there's a strong sense that the old girl is very happy to be in good hands.

Castlepoint homestead in August 2000.
Sketch by Des De Stefano/Wairarapa Archive

Because the homestead *is* an old girl — her core is over 100 years old — she's had additions over the years and now sports a mixture of very sophisticated technology, including a state-of-the-art air-conditioned office, and some intriguing antique furniture that looks, paradoxically, both out of place and entirely at home. Like most long-standing farming operations, the homestead has always been central to the station — the hearth and the beating heart of the place — and in order to understand Castlepoint in the twenty-first century, you need to know about the homestead.

To access the upstairs office, built in the 1980s, a motorized invalid's lift has been installed and a new roofed-over lap pool added, some of the few concessions to Emily Crofoot's multiple sclerosis, along with her crutch-holder that's been welded to the side of her four-wheel-drive Yamaha Rhino 700. You could say it's been customized. Other farmers might use something similar for a shepherd's stick, but here it serves another purpose entirely. No one makes a big deal of it, and Emily won't let it be a big deal: 'It's my reality.' She certainly doesn't let it define her, and it doesn't stop her participating fully in the management of her farm. There's a lot of quiet courage in this family.

The man doing the painting is known to everyone as Jolly, although his real name is Graham McConaghty. He moved to Castlepoint a few years ago and has stayed on, as general handyman and truck driver. He also mows lawns for many of the holiday homes in the settlement, a task he took over when 'Old Mr Heaps'

The view back towards Castle Point Lighthouse and across the Quarters Paddock, once the home of the shepherds and cooks who lived and worked on the station.

was poorly, and never stopped. Eric Heaps, who passed away in 2010, was the last cowman/gardener employed at Castlepoint Station. Jolly's partner, Rhonda, helps out with the housekeeping at the homestead and is also a relief cleaner at the holiday park. Stu Neal is the farm manager, and his wife, Ginny Neal, the principal release teacher at Whareama School, is also the station's health and safety officer — because that's the way it works around here: it's a family place, first and foremost.

There's a beautiful garden again, put in since Emily Crofoot has been here — minus the overhead powerlines, which have all been buried, so when you're sitting at the kitchen table there's nothing to obscure your view of the lighthouse and the headland on the horizon.

Deep-blue glazed pots of fragrant herbs march down the steps to a lawn where fat quail feed in the early morning light, oblivious of the house cat and the little brown-and-white dog curled up in her basket. There's a small kitchen garden out the other side of the house, with raised beds of serious man-sized tomatoes — none of those fiddly cocktail things here — and lettuces, although the huge vegetable gardens and the old orchards that used to fill the shelves with preserves are long gone.

Two local women look after the garden: its designer and loving caretaker for many years, Jill Maunsell, who pops in to mow the lawns with her dog and ride-on mower, and neighbour Heather Weyde, who comes in a couple of days a week to help maintain the new gardens. Like any garden, there's always weeding and watering, and because this is Castlepoint, lots of mulching, with thick layers of pea-straw nestled between the plants to conserve every precious drop. Masses of pink and white roses shelter behind a new high fence, and now that there's a touch of autumn in the crisp air, spent blooms hang heavy and thick above a wonderful blend of old-fashioned flowers and modern cultivars. Emily Crofoot loves pink, blue and white, and her garden reflects that, with a colourful blend of belladonna lilies, alstroemeria, fuchsia, pelargoniums, white begonias, dahlias, aquilegia, salvia, heliotrope, iris, penstemon, sweet william, lavender and day-lilies.

Inside the house the day-lilies are echoed vividly in a large watercolour of Emily and Anders' home, Locust Brook Cottage, at Braewold, their previous farm back in Mount Kisco, in New York State. It was painted for the Crofoots by a family friend, and it shows a lush landscape, with a large dark-green farmhouse, that you know instantly isn't in New Zealand. Although the shapes are different, the feeling is the same — a much-loved family farm.

On the front doorstep of the homestead is what at first appears to be an anomaly — a huge chunk of rose quartz, looking surprisingly reminiscent of Castle Rock. There's also an apricot-coloured vireya rhododendron in a half wine barrel, but your eye is drawn back to the huge chunk of crystal sitting quietly to your right. Known universally as the love stone, rose quartz is supposed to add positive energy to relationships and to promote harmony, compassion and forgiveness, enhancing self-confidence and creativity. While the Crofoot family have those qualities in abundance, that's not the reason it's here.

The crystal was quarried in Bedford, at a neighbouring farm to the one where Emily grew up, in Westchester County, New York State. It came to New Zealand with the family, when Braewold, which had been in Emily's family for generations, was sold. It's almost as if the bedrock that created this family is here for the world to see, and, like all of us, it's another migrant to Aotearoa.

The first thing you notice inside the hallway is Emily's piano, piled high with sheet music and prayer books — testament to her lifelong love of liturgical music — along with her reading glasses. The second thing you notice is the beautiful wooden heart of the old house, stretching the length of the building and opening out to more roses and star-jasmine out the back door. The hallway is high and wide, and it doesn't take much to imagine generations of children running along it; there has even been a published description of children pulling their Buzzy

Bees behind them *clack, clack, clack* along the wooden floors, which is about as Kiwiana as it comes. Now the hall is lined with huge quilts and wall-hangings, which indicate another of Emily's passions: hand crafts.

As well as being a farmer, Emily Crofoot is also an accomplished textile artist, and the massive cream wall-hanging on the right is one of hers. It took two fleeces, which she spun herself before weaving what was intended to be a bedspread. By the time it was finished, it was way too heavy for this climate, and instead graces the walls of Castlepoint, a place where a good fleece has always been valued.

There's also a large blue-and-white quilt purchased in the Amish country, and an American wedding quilt that was made for the Crofoots, a colourful collage featuring, not surprisingly, fields, crops, horses and cattle. And just in case you're not getting the full picture, in the dining room, which also doubles as a boardroom and venue for business meetings, as well as the electronic whiteboard, two extraordinary pieces of textile art are featured, in pride of place — one over the fireplace, and one over the sideboard. Both are by renowned Christchurch artist the late Vivienne Mountfort, who completed the works while in her eighties, two years before her death in 2004, after visits to the station and many detailed discussions with Emily as to the best view and form for the works. Both are made of felted wool; each one is composed of three stitched panels depicting an aspect of the station — one featuring the lighthouse, the other Castle Rock — and each is a powerful and compelling piece of art.

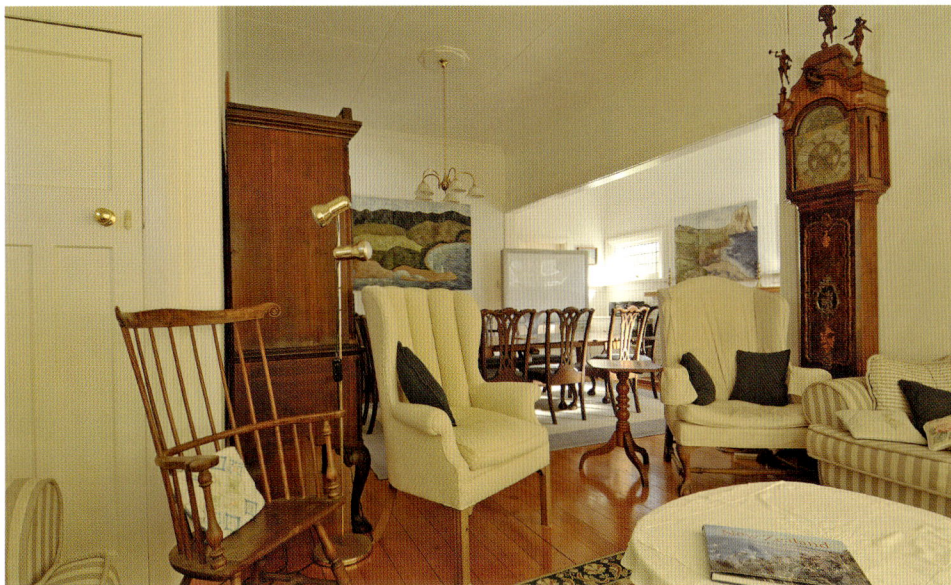

Opposite page: The 100-year-old wooden core of the homestead, lined with Emily's own hand-woven quilts and wall-hangings.

Left: The dining room and board-room, equipped with electronic whiteboard, antique furniture and textile art by New Zealand artist Vivienne Mountfort.

That this place has always inspired artists goes without saying: the paintings on the walls of the homestead include a Peter Williams oil of the famous beach races and a series of monochromes by Peter Scaife showing the loading of bales of wool from the old narrow jetty and a team of eight bullocks. They've been recently joined by a new painting, by yet another visitor, and that won't be the last. Everyone tries to capture Castlepoint — from eminent photographers such as Brian Brake and Ans Westra to every tourist and holidaymaker — but it's too big for most cameras; the land too rich in layers of meaning to be captured by any single medium.

The furniture includes some impressively old antiques that look different to a Kiwi eye, because they came over from the States with the Crofoots. They include what can only be described as a great-grandfather clock, its magnificence topped with a carved Atlas bearing the weight of the world, flanked by bare-breasted angels and their trumpets. Together with wonderful heavy wooden dressers and chests of drawers, these are the 'old friends' that Emily's parents, Jim and

Twink Wood, joke about coming to visit, and were shipped to New Zealand when Braewold was finally sold. It's another grounding link. The old pieces are now well and truly at home, so Jim can say without irony that they can come visit their furniture and it's like old times.

Like most farms, the kitchen table is where things are discussed; only these days that's usually with laptops open, and iPhones out. It's also where newspapers are read and daily programmes coordinated, with Holly, the three-year-old Jack Russell and unofficial Mayor of Castlepoint Station, either watching from a convenient lap or curled up in her basket by the door.

In a concession to his previous life working in a restaurant, Anders Crofoot has a coffee machine and makes a mean cup of 'proper' coffee. While previous farm wives might wonder about that, along with the chef's salads and corn puddings on the menu, they'd have no problem with the superb roast beef, bacon-and-egg pie or the Anzac biscuits whipped up for a meeting round the table to discuss the upcoming pasture-planting schedule with the agronomist.

The library, on the way to the upstairs office, shows a similar blend of cultures and influences — from the old leather-bound dictionaries of architecture and engineering to reference books on subjects as diverse as physics, maths, computing, economics, biomimicry and management, all sharing shelf space with popular novels and books on animal husbandry, *War and Peace*, *All Creatures Great and Small* and a whole section devoted to children's books such as *Mary Poppins* and *Pippi Longstocking*, along with English classics like CS Lewis's *The Chronicles of Narnia* and collections by Roald Dahl interspersed with American children's series and stories by local New Zealand authors like Ken Catran.

The office is the air-conditioned working hub, containing several computer workstations and piles of reports, printouts and business papers. It sits at the top of the house in an upstairs addition. It's an important part of the business, and a visual reminder of how multiskilled the Crofoots are and what a multidisciplinary business it is running a modern sheep and beef property the size and scale of Castlepoint these days.

Back downstairs, in the room behind the kitchen there is something from Anders' family in Omaha, Nebraska — a Kiwi would call it a meat safe, but he calls it a pie safe. Whatever the name, the purpose is the same and it's a beautiful old piece of working furniture with pierced metal facings. It's still part of a busy farm as well as being a tangible reminder of the linking together of multiple cultures, which is the mark of a nation of migrants, something Castlepoint has always been very good at recognizing.

The same room provides a snapshot of a working farm, including a massive chest freezer, its layers of contents neatly categorized in a handwritten list taped to the lid. The piles of hats, boots, jackets and labelled keys, along with heaps of notebooks, a sink and stacks of towels with industrial-size containers of sunscreen and pumice handcleaner, are a dead giveaway that Castlepoint is a no-nonsense farm — and the clear, laminated fire instructions and labelled emergency exits and procedures show too that they take their jobs, and their responsibilities, seriously.

While Holly spends a lot of time indoors with the family, she's no lap-dog, and her kennel sits outside the back door, where there's also a stack of firewood split for the wood-burner sitting in the corner of the kitchen, a reminder that while those high ceilings make the rooms cool in summer, winter and wooden floors are another story.

Most of all, there is a strong sense that this is a family home, and not just for the Crofoots; the sense of family at Castlepoint extends out into the community and across the station, something that all close-knit rural communities would recognize but which has a special resonance at Castlepoint. There's also a strong sense of continuing a very old story here — and not just because Emily's family had been working the land for generations before Thomas Guthrie, the founder of Castlepoint Station, brought his first flock of merinos over from Wellington. There's a strong perception that the land is back with a family again — that the story of farming people coming here to find a better life for their children is being repeated; and it's a story that Castlepoint Station knows and understands.

It's a family place again.

The late Peter Scaife's depiction of wool-loading at the Castlepoint jetty, from which the first wool clips were sent to Wellington from Castlepoint and much of the Wairarapa.
Peter Scaife

Enduring land, capricious weather

It all begins and ends with the land — and an ancient story of earthquake, upheaval and tectonic movement plays close to the surface at Castlepoint Station. Long and narrow, the station is the result of a constant battle between land and sea, her coastal soils lashed by rain, baked by sun and eroded by relentless wind and waves. But her cliffs stand against the sea like a bastion — and the looming edifice of Castle Rock, with the encircling arm of the reef and the omnipresent lighthouse, guard her well.

HERE, IT ALL STARTS WITH THE LAND. While every place can claim to be unique in some way, Castlepoint Station has a distinctive feel about it that is like no other place on earth.

A prosaic description would discuss how the effects of wind erosion on limestone over a great deal of time has produced Castle Rock, the area's most distinctive local landmark. Beneath this lies a small beachside settlement on the Wairarapa coast, nowadays an hour's drive northeast of Masterton, its nearest urban neighbour. However, such a description would miss the reality of the place by the proverbial country mile, and do a complete disservice to the staggeringly beautiful scenery that wraps itself from horizon to horizon. In high summer it is a panoramic spread of blue, gold and dusty brown, and in winter a breathtaking ringside seat to the spectacle of land versus sea, when huge waves batter the cliffs and horizontal rain lashes everything foolish enough to be outside.

No description can ever prepare you for the breathtaking magnificence of Castlepoint itself: the rock jutting up, clearly half of what it once was, with one side eaten into by wind and sea and the other still covered in soil, toetoe and long grasses and, at the right time of year, with the air full of the incessant summer song of cicadas. On the beach there are massive rocks in the curve below Castle Rock, and a wide sweeping arc of the finest sand you can imagine, sparkling in the sun, with the Pacific Ocean pounding through the gap and swirling into the lagoon sheltered by the rocks and the encircling reef. Some say the reef looks like a man on his side; to others it resembles nothing so much as a submarine — what no one can deny is that its formation determined the history of this area.

Castlepoint's amazing physical location is a major part of its attraction, and has provided many of the not inconsiderable hurdles that those who chose to live here have been forced to overcome. While some well-known Kiwi stations have cold and snow along with searing heat to make them strong, and others deal with isolation, floods and drought, many of Castlepoint's unique challenges come from the sea. The significant impact of the station's maritime location should never be underestimated. You only have to turn towards the sound of the ocean — it's never far away.

Sited on a dangerous and unpredictable section of coast, historically the property was centred around a spectacular and utterly distinctive natural formation, a towering rocky promontory 162 metres above sea level. Those who knew about such things found it reminiscent of a castle and its battlements, while to everyone else Castle Rock was a great lookout as well as providing a navigation point visible from a long distance. It also signalled a safe harbour, the reef protecting a placid lagoon and a long, sandy beach stretching out to the north.

Previous page: An unmistakable scene — Castle Point Lighthouse fixed in the limestone reef, guarding an austere coastline and battling Pacific swells.

Opposite page, top: The landscape from the grassy side of Castle Rock, 162 metres high, jutting out into the ocean.

Bottom: The sea finds a way through a recess in the reef, flowing into the lagoon.

Beyond are low hills and dry slopes, and even more beaches, with rocks and a dramatic cavern beneath towering cliffs, where breathtaking views inevitably draw the eye out over the wide reaches of the Pacific Ocean in its many guises.

Today, eyes that look out to sea here are likely to be checking out the waves — not with a view to landing cargo or taking on board bales of wool, but as a reflection of Castlepoint's current status as a Mecca for surfers, drawn to the area by its amazing waves which break onto some stunning beaches.

This incredibly beautiful area now forms part of the Department of Conservation's Castlepoint Scenic Reserve, purchased for the nation in the mid 'seventies. For many years this land was integral to the heart of the station and the surrounding area. In much earlier days, long before roads, the safe anchorage provided a gateway to the opening up of the hinterland and was an important stage in the sea passage north, from Wellington to Napier in the Hawke's Bay.

What many people don't realize, when they look at this astounding land and seascape, is that they are also looking at a key to understanding the ancient prehistory lying just below the surface, and which played an important part in making the area so visually distinctive.

Together with Castle Rock, the narrow limestone reef forms the Castlepoint Formation, largely composed of broken barnacles and the skeletal remains of marine life deposited offshore during the most recent ice age, over two million years ago. If you want to see examples of the fossils themselves, today most of the best are on the exposed northern reef, which also happens to be the most dangerous part, especially during high swells and rough weather.

Looking back from the seaward side you can clearly see what happens when strong prevailing currents build up layers of seashells and shelly sand — with larger grains than regular sand and recognizable shell fragments — and crushed rock. Powerful swells then erode the softer crushed rock in the reef at a faster rate, leaving behind the much harder limestone. The result is a landscape resembling something from another planet.

From the sea, you can observe how Castle Rock is constructed from layers of limestone laid over grey siltstone. The siltstone is a much older material, by a good three million years, and was formed in much deeper water. Scientists tell us that at one time, Castle Rock stood at roughly double its present size; but at some stage, a very long time ago, it was broken in two, with one side completely reclaimed by the sea. When you stand on the beach and look across at the rock, it becomes immediately apparent and is utterly awe-inspiring, while the view from directly below, looking up at the sheer face, can make your head spin.

Opposite page: Exposed scallop fossils and shell fragments in the walls of the reef at Castlepoint.

More than seventy different fossil species have been recorded on the reef, many of them creatures long since extinct, and one of the most telling finds is a variety of scallop which today survives only in the much colder waters of Otago. What this tells us is that at the time the scallop was alive, the waters off Castlepoint were much colder than they are today. As a result, scientists now believe the limestone there was formed during a period of climate change, when the temperature of the surrounding sea warmed from cool to temperate. This may have been caused by one of two things — either a retreat of the Antarctic ice-sheet or a significant shift in ocean currents. Either way, a dramatic change in water temperature was produced, sufficient to completely change the marine population living off the Wairarapa coast. Nowadays, the scallops have all gone but there are paua and crayfish enough to make gathering seafood worthwhile. Fortunately, the rough and unpredictable weather acts to some degree to protect those same resources from the poaching that is stripping the coast elsewhere.

The area is also close to both the Wairarapa Fault, to the west, and a gigantic undersea region of tectonic subduction to the east, which runs the length of New Zealand and beyond. Here the Australian and Pacific plates grind against each other, part of the great Pacific Rim of Fire. That this circle of instability brings earthquakes, volcanic activity and tsunami to countries bordering the Pacific Ocean is a geological fact of life, on a grand scale, as the tragic events of February 2011 in Canterbury and March 2011 in Japan have proved. On a much smaller scale, the effect for Castlepoint is that, over thousands of years, small but persistent upward shifts eventually took the limestone reef from the seabed all the way up to the surface. At the same time, repeated movement of major faultlines on either side meant that the reef which formed remained narrow and elongated instead of spreading out and becoming broader. While current monitoring hasn't recorded any recent activity on these faultlines, it's worth remembering that geological time operates on a vastly different scale to human time, and this area remains an active part of the Earth's crust. What this means is that what you see now won't necessarily always be there.

The same dynamic is apparent in the rocks on the reef itself, their whimsical shapes taking irregularity to an extreme. These are the result of the base limestone being first lifted into the air and then exposed to long-term wind and water erosion. Imagine a time-exposure camera able to record on a geological timescale, and then fast-forward — you'd see the wind and sea rapidly eating their way into the rocks, burrowing into the softer layers and repelled for a while by the harder ones — leaving behind incredible shapes and extraordinary rock sculptures, each completely different from its neighbour.

Razor-like rocks at Whakataki, looking south to
Castlepoint. The strange formation is evidence
of resistant rock beds, standing up as ridges,
and less resistant rock cut out by sea and wind
forming narrow gutters.

Tsunami

The waterfront at Castlepoint and the track up to the new station woolshed, perched high and close to the airstrip, are clearly marked with distinctive crisp blue-and-white tsunami warning signs, with their stylized waves chasing a human figure up the side of a mountain. They can look rather ironic, especially against a dry summer background.

They've been put there for a very good reason. There's nothing much between Castlepoint and the eastern side of the Pacific, and the station and settlement are linked in through Civil Defence to the Pacific Tsunami Monitoring System. The

lighthouse houses one of New Zealand's fourteen mainland tsunami gauges, which monitor tsunamis caused by distant earthquake events. While that's reassuring in one sense, it's not much good for local events, as they would typically occur and arrive before scientists would have time to issue a warning.

When the sirens go, everyone is evacuated up the hill to the woolshed, as happened one morning at 5 a.m., following an earthquake in South America. Jim Wood describes being woken in the middle of the night and making the journey up the hill, where everyone sat around drinking cups of coffee and waiting for the all-clear. While the area is exposed to a 'big one' on the flats, the hills are very close and the evacuation procedures well rehearsed. Castlepoint Station is a local coordinator, along with the holiday park managers. While they were contacted and placed on standby by Masterton Civil Defence during the March 2011 Pacific-wide tsunami alert following the tragic events in Japan, fortunately no evacuation was required.

There's nothing new about tsunami alerts, really. Taffy Williams, who was a keeper at the Castle Point Lighthouse from 1958 to 1961, describes one time he

Opposite page: One of the many tsunami evacuation signs posted along the exposed Castlepoint coast.

Left: Bullish waves surge against the reef and flood The Gap during an easterly storm.

and his wife were in Masterton, putting in their grocery order. A woman told them there'd been a tidal wave on the east coast and Castlepoint was under water. 'We raced back lickety-split to discover everything pretty normal. The area had been put on high alert because of an unusually high tide. We had visions of never seeing our children again. We were told that an alarm would sound that night and if it did we were to run to the hills. We kept having visions of it all gone, the lighthouse included.'

Fortunately it didn't happen, and the lighthouse is still there.

Another distinctive geological feature of Castlepoint is the Cave of Muturangi's Octopus, which runs beneath the lighthouse. While not visible from the main beach, at low tide the western entrance is accessible by foot. Over hundreds of years, the sea has eaten away a nine-metre-high cavern, used for social gatherings by fur seals and humans alike.

In common with the rest of eastern Wairarapa, most of the rock beneath Castlepoint Station and its coastline is sedimentary, formed when sediments washed off the land and into the ocean over the past 80 million years. These have since been lifted above sea level as New Zealand gradually rose out of the sea, pushed up by tectonic plate activity to the east.

To geologists, the area from the mouth of the Mataikona River in the north to the Whareama River in the south is known as the Whakataki Formation, a zone of rock structures and graded beds up to 2 kilometres wide. The Whakataki Formation dominates the geology of the coastline here, and is best seen at low tide, in the area south of Castle Rock and at Christmas Bay. There the sea pulls back to expose long, uniform, razor-like rows of rock lining the foreshore. Further inland, parts of the same geological formation, with similarly distinctive rocks, lie exposed on ridge crests, in the sides of steep streams and in several of the small quarries sited on Castlepoint Station. These quarries are now used as a supply of rotten rock, soft, friable and perfect for converting into metal for the internal roading system and the laneway, a vital internal arterial road linking all parts of the station.

For much of its prehistory, Castlepoint, along with most of the rest of the Wairarapa, was densely forested. However, climate change brought a prolonged cycle of drought followed by devastating fires which swept through the area, aided by the strong winds the region is famous for, leaving behind the regenerating fern and light manuka and kanuka scrub which greeted the first European settlers.

The resulting soil picture at Castlepoint is one of mostly sedimentary soils, a characteristic of land which has been uplifted from the ocean and subsequently eroded by high winds. There is relatively little topsoil and not a lot of organic matter, which is one of the reasons why these hills dry off so quickly. The parent material also has a very high clay content, and when the cleared land was cultivated by tractor and plough, it created a hard pan beneath the surface; in some places only 45 centimetres below. In layperson's terms, as the ploughshare turned the top part of the soil, it also pressed on and compacted the bottom layer, creating the hard pan that subsequent farmers have had to deal with.

Opposite page: Metal scars from the dogged weather at Castlepoint.

The thin soils here are particularly vulnerable to erosion, with poor water-holding capacity meaning they dry out quickly in summer but become quite wet in winter. This in turn creates the danger of soil slippage, when the fully saturated top later eventually becomes too heavy for the clay underneath and it slides. Around five years ago, Castlepoint Station saw about 150 millimetres of rain in just three hours. The resulting slips left scarring on the hills that remains to this day, and a whole fence line was washed out in a matter of hours. Like other East Coast properties, Castlepoint Station is working with the Greater Wellington Regional Council on this issue, and their soil conservation plan has seen the planting of up to 2000 poplar and willow poles a year in an attempt to stabilize the areas most prone to slipping. Each pole is wrapped in an ingenious plastic sleeve, which protects the young trunk from browsing stock by the very nature of its smoothness — there's no satisfaction for an animal trying to scratch an itch, for a start — and as the trunk expands, the sleeve is designed to burst naturally. There's also an added benefit, with the new trees providing welcome additional summer shade and shelter for the stock. Because 'back then', when they cleared the land of scrub and gorse they took out *everything* — it was easier, and that was the way things were done then — but it did leave behind some very bare hills, vulnerable to erosion and baking hot in the sun.

And that brings us to the other thing you usually notice right away at Castlepoint — the infamous wind. The Department of Conservation has recorded wind speeds at Castlepoint exceeding 200 kilometres an hour, and while this isn't an everyday occurrence, the area has recorded more than its fair share of winds reaching gale or hurricane force. The prevailing wind is from the northwest and comes funnelling through the Manawatu Gorge, roaring out here to where the Met Service leases the site for one of their automated weather stations.

Anders Crofoot came here in 1998 and will tell you how he grew up sailing all his life, in Long Island Sound and at his grandparents' place in Maine, as well as doing quite a bit of deep-water racing: 'And I *thought* I knew what wind was until I arrived here. We looked out over the bay and it was white with spray which had to be 12 metres high. Our first month at Castlepoint, the wind averaged 45 kilometres an hour all month, with a peak of 97 kilometres an hour.' It was October and the spring equinox — and a taste of things to come. 'In most areas, you come out of winter when the grass growth would steadily increase throughout the spring, but what we found was that growth would stop for a while in October, the grass basically ducks for shelter, then picks up again. Unfortunately, this is right when the ewes are feeding their lambs and you want as much grass as you can get.'

People will tell you that Castlepoint gets a bad press because of the weather station, but the reality is everyone has a wind story at Castlepoint, and these are impressive.

While the strong winds usually come from the northwest, the biggest storms come from the east, producing violent surges capable of shifting surface rock and sand. On occasion, this force tears large chunks of rock from the reef itself and leaves deep recesses for the incoming sea to exploit.

Mind you, the wind isn't *all* bad. For one thing, it helps keep the stock healthy, blowing away all the facial eczema spores before they can do much damage. In another example, one Wellington family came to work at the station on medical recommendation, as an ideal environment for their young daughter. The poor girl suffered from chronic asthma and associated breathing difficulties. Within weeks of arriving at the station, she was breathing normally again, enjoying the benefit of Castlepoint's cleaner, and certainly faster-moving, air.

Further inland, the wind buffets sand, seaside uplands and rocky outcrops alike. Above these, a shallow layer of precious topsoil lies over much harder sandstone, producing the erosion-prone hills which need to be carefully managed, in common with much of New Zealand's East Coast.

In farming terms Castlepoint is a summer-dry station, which means it receives most of its rainfall in the winter months and the summers can often be extremely dry — as the tawny slopes testify, looking for all the world like the flanks of a dusty lion as they recede into the horizon in shades of brown and gold.

While seaborne storms can wreak havoc in the winter, its seaside location also works to save Castlepoint Station from the worst of the cold weather, with average winter temperatures much milder than over the hills in the Wairarapa Valley. There are relatively few frosts, although snow isn't completely unknown, falling mostly on the hilltops, the highest of which is 270 metres above sea level. However, on some memorable occasions, it's been cold enough for snow to blanket the ground *at* sea level.

Millennia in the making, and at the mercy of the sea and the wind, on a clear summer's day Castlepoint can be paradise. So what if things can change at a moment's notice, as another storm rolls in? It's Castlepoint, where bracing weather is a fact of life, and life is good.

Volatile seas off the reef, a popular shore-fishing location despite the regularity of accidents and, over the years, a great number of fatalities owing to the deep currents.

Sand piled high against the reef.

Tangata whenua, people of the land

That the tangata whenua arrived here can be blamed on a mischievous octopus — that they remained, a tribute to their mana. It was never a densely populated area, and those who chose to live here were strong. Undaunted by the capricious weather and able to work with its many moods, they survived earthquake, fire and the bloodshed of history to make their living from the land's slopes, bays and rocky shores.

Previous page: Rippled sand at low tide in the bay at Castlepoint.

KUPE'S ARRIVAL, WHETHER IT WAS HOT ON THE HEELS of a bait-thieving octopus or fleeing from a jealous husband — a racier alternative version of the discovery legend — is generally supposed to have occurred in the thirteenth century. While the event itself is so far in the past that determining accurate dates and figures is impossible, some accounts have Kupe at the head of an occupying party of seventy. Through local legend and whakapapa, Kupe's voyage of discovery can be traced from Northland to the Wairarapa, with his descendants described by some as this country's first human inhabitants.

Those same legends disagree about the origin of the Maori name for the area: Rangiwhakaoma, where the sky runs. Some say it's a vivid and poetic description of Kupe's amazing voyage south from the mythical homeland of Hawaiki. Others have it as the name of a gigantic sleeping man whose head can be seen in the seaward side of Castle Rock, his body forming the sheltering reef; yet others claim that Rangiwhakaoma was a man of flesh and blood, left behind by Kupe to retain his presence, or vital fire, on the land.

Whatever the truth — and who can say what's true and what's not after so much time has passed — tradition has it that within two generations of Kupe's epic journey another great ocean-going waka, *Kurahaupo*, and its captain, Whatonga, set out from Hawaiki to retrace his path. The party landed at a place they called Matirie, believed to be where the lighthouse stands today. Whatonga had two sons, Tara and Tautoki, whose descendants settled what we now know as the Wairarapa and Wellington, eventually calling themselves Rangitane, after Tautoki's son. The iwi thrived, and spread along the East Coast as far as Hawke's Bay, as well as through the Manawatu and Horowhenua.

During the climatically and geographically turbulent sixteenth century, which saw several natural disasters, most of the growing population moved inland and down to the South Island. This left the coastal areas to those content to live a semi-nomadic life between seasonal coastal fishing sites and more permanent freshwater villages beside river banks and inlets. During the often harsh winters, when violent storms lashed the coast and made fishing much more difficult and unreliable, the people moved further inland.

During the eighteenth century Ngati Kahungunu joined the Rangitane in the Castlepoint area, as Kahungunu's diplomatically astute descendant Te Huki extended his iwi's influence from Poverty Bay to the Wairarapa through a series of strategic marital alliances. The end result of all those marriages was known as Te Huki's Net, and saw the creation of Ngati Kahungunu ki Wairarapa, whose occupation today stretches along the whole of the Wairarapa coastline.

Certainly, the earliest inhabitants to lay claim to authority over land and sea at Castlepoint were the Rangitane, through the paramount hapu or subtribe, Ngati Hamua. They were later joined by Te Hika o Papauma, from Ngati Kahungunu. Traditionally, Ngati Hamua's influence extended into the main valley of the Wairarapa while Te Hika o Papauma controlled the area from Whareama to Akitio, and as far inland as Tinui and the Puketoi Range.

For the most part, there was peaceful coexistence around Castlepoint and Mataikona, although a sandstone plinth along the Mataikona road commemorates the end of a famous battle. The years that followed inevitably saw intermarriage mingle the bloodlines in a way that made warfare less of an option, and coexistence much more practical.

The peace lasted until 1819–1822, when the southern Wairarapa iwi were confronted first by musket-wielding Ngapuhi and their allies from the north, and then by Ngati Toa from the west. For the next ten years the local inhabitants were harried and pushed into refuge in the Mahia Peninsula and what later became known as Seventy Mile Bush. By 1840, when this turbulent period finally came to an end, the Maori population of the entire Wairarapa was approximately 800, with only a relative handful still living around Castlepoint and Mataikona.

Today, Maori who claim the Castlepoint area as their turangawaewae, or rightful place, are the descendants of one of two famous eighteenth-century ancestors — Tamahau Te Rangiwhakaewa, of Ngati Hamua, and Te Matau, of Te Hika o Papauma, through the Maaka and Potangaroa families.

Of necessity, this is a simplified account of what was a much more complex and detailed history, with all the subtleties and complexities you would expect to find as strategic allegiances formed, shifted and re-formed again over many generations and people coped with dramatic changes to their lives. The prehistoric record held in the land itself, as well as the oral histories passed down through the generations, tell of an untrustworthy landscape that produced high winds, drought and destructive earthquakes. In addition, powerful socio-political tides swept through the human population as disruptive new influences, such as colonizing Europeans and the musket, created intense competition for the basic requirements of human survival — land, food and fresh water.

Land rights are never simple, and they certainly were not here, where every bay, inlet and river was typically used at one time by one hapu and at other times by another, and in between by relatives of both. Human history everywhere has been a series of land disputes, one way or another. This part of the world is no exception.

What is indisputable, however, is the archaeological record, which provides clear evidence, some of which is still visible today, of various pa sites along the coast. These are particularly noticeable at Mataikona, where the presence of karaka and kowhai trees strongly suggest seasonal villages. While poisonous in their natural state, the bright-yellow karaka berries contain a tough seed that can, after careful and knowledgeable preparation, provide a smooth, edible flesh. Early Maori valued this as an additional food source, and karaka trees were cultivated over time, surviving to the present day to provide confirmation of permanent occupation. In addition, over the years numerous Maori artefacts have been found up and down the coast, at Waimimi, Otahome, Castlepoint, Whakataki and Mataikona.

For more than forty years, Masterton jeweller and keen local historian Keith Cairns made a valuable and detailed study of early Maori occupation of the Wairarapa. His prodigious efforts include writing to practically every farmer in the region, requesting information about old Maori sites on their land. While an enthusiastic amateur, his work was later taken up by teams of trained archaeologists and local Maori, who have investigated some of the sites Keith was able to pinpoint. In addition, time has unearthed numerous skeletons, which have been subsequently identified as Whatonga ancestors before being re-interred; surely the ultimate physical evidence of a coastal lineage of Maori occupation stretching back some 700 years.

Opposite page, top: A cloaked Maori figure and a European at Deliverance Cove. *Collection of the Hawke's Bay Cultural Trust — Hawke's Bay Museum*

Bottom: Castlepoint during the time of the New Zealand wars, in the 1860s. *Wairarapa Archive*

Left: A gentle meeting of land and sea, the lagoon beyond the entrance to Deliverance Cove.

The shores of Castlepoint at dawn, Maori fishing grounds
for over 700 years.

PLAN
of the
WAIRARAPA
District &c.

Ruamanga Range

Wanganui District

Wanganui

Fine Level Country

Rangitiki

Swampy

Fern Valley

Manawatu

Swampy

Horowenua

THICKLY TIMBERED

Very Hilly

Ohau

Otaki

Good Grazing

Fern Ground

Maia Roon

E. Settlement

Very heavy Bush

Very high Ranges

CASTLE POINT

Remutaka

VALLEY

Fine Country

Open Country

Mana

Good Grazing

Motuawaka

COOKS

Palliser Hd.

Pidvalla

Very heavy timbered

Waiata Lake

Good Grazing

Cotter St.

Vansecour St.

Mr Masters

Good Grazing

W. Shoar

Good Land

Kelley

Greentown

Watotapa

S. Settlement

PALLISER

Oherepunga

Very high Hill

BAY

Te Kopi

WHALING STATION

Otakawa

Ohae

Ohau Settlement

KUKAWAWAHUI

Cape Palliser

STRAITS

W. Kingmister
Land Surveyor Dept.
Wellington

Early European settlement

Determination to find a better life on the other side of the world brought European colonization to the East Coast, where sheer hard work created an immense sheep farm out of the bush. They were tough times and the people who came to the end of the earth had to be resilient to weather the new land they found, and learn to make a virtue out of necessity. They gave their hearts to it, as well as some of their children, as only the strong would survive the process by which Castlepoint became a thriving station and a close-knit community.

THE FIRST EUROPEANS TO SET FOOT AT CASTLEPOINT wasted no time in thanking the Lord for providing a safe anchorage along an otherwise godforsaken coast.

It was 1 November 1843 and a confusion of Williams was travelling north from Wellington to Gisborne in the schooner *Columbine* — two missionaries, William Colenso, whose name history would choose to remember, and a Mr William Williams and his son Leonard Williams. The vessel had been caught out by bad weather, and sought refuge in the only natural harbour between Hawke's Bay and Wellington, promptly naming it Deliverance Cove, for obvious reasons.

Another five years would blow by before Castlepoint Station would make its tentative beginnings. Colenso would continue to make intermittent visits as he travelled up and down the coast, ministering to his far-flung flock and reporting

Previous page: An early survey of Wairarapa region in 1845, marking the first stations and settlements, as well as areas with potential for grazing.
Alexander Turnbull Library, 2739

Right: Mataikona bullock team at the end of the 1800s.
Wairarapa Archive

on the prospects of settlement for the growing colony. Another visitor was the enterprising FA Weld, later to become a significant landowner in the Wairarapa Valley. However, Mr Weld deemed the land at Castlepoint unsuitable for farming, describing the flats as swamp-ridden. Ironically, this same land, when drained and sown by future farmers, was destined to become some of the most fertile and productive on the property.

It took a determined young Englishman from the Isle of Wight to prove Weld wrong. When Thomas Guthrie first set eyes on what would become Castlepoint Station, he'd been in the colony for seven years and was living in Wellington with his wife, Ann, and four young children. Three of those had been born there, their parents and older sister having survived the obligatory sea passage from England, with its associated difficulties. While their journey was typical of many and not as difficult as some, it was nevertheless a 'colonial rite of passage', forever separating the colonists from those they left behind and marking them with strong memories as it winnowed the weak from the strong.

Thomas Guthrie, then twenty-five, along with Ann and their firstborn daughter were typical of the 800 immigrants enticed to the new colony by the New Zealand Company, established by Edward Gibbon Wakefield — surveyor, land agent, social engineer and, at one point in his turbulent career, infamous as the scandalous abductor of a young heiress. In his efforts to fill the new land with immigrants, Wakefield had described their destination glowingly: 'fittest in the world for colonization, as the most beautiful country with the finest climate, and the most productive soil'.

Castlepoint Station stock yards, killing shed and woolshed near the shore, circa 1910.
Laing family collection

Thomas met the Company's advertised criteria, which called for 'Mechanics, Gardeners, and Agricultural Labourers, being married and not exceeding 30 years of age', and signed up for free passage to a better life. In 1839 the Guthries set out for the other side of the world, leaving behind everything they had known, which by now included an uncertain economic future as the effects of the Industrial Revolution began to bite, threatening farm wages and those with traditional skills.

Their ship was the *Adelaide*, one of the initial three New Zealand Company ships, and their journey took 176 days. Just two days into the voyage a violent storm washed all the livestock overboard, forcing the passengers and crew to endure a monotonous diet of salted beef and pickled pork until they reached Cape Town.

The *Adelaide* would finally arrive in Wellington and dock at Port Nicholson on 7 March 1840 — to a very inauspicious beginning. A fierce storm, lightning, gale-force winds and flooding greeted them, and with few other options, the young family was forced to make a home for themselves in the fledgling settlement. Thomas found work as a dairyman, and the family lived on Willis Street for seven years, no closer to their dream of prosperity and a rural life.

Three more children were born before Thomas senior went north into the Wairarapa to negotiate the lease of a tract of land at Rangiwhakaoma — what is now known as Castlepoint. The deal was for 30,000 acres, for which in 1847 Guthrie agreed an initial annual rent of £69, which by 1851 had increased to £200 — a figure cited in official proceedings when the issue of Native Land leases was debated.

At the time, European immigrants were engaged in widespread and usually informal leasing arrangements with local Maori. They were desperate to find large parcels of land expansive enough to graze sheep. Due to Castlepoint's extreme isolation, Guthrie's deal never received any official sort of proclamation, unlike most other such land leases at the time. The first record of his arrangement came two months later, in the form of an advertisement for his new station, in the *Wellington Independent*, offering to take in cattle 'on reasonable terms'.

Further record of Guthrie's progress came in 1848 from Charles Pharazyn, at Palliser Bay's Whatarangi Station. In his diary entry for 18 April, Pharazyn noted that Guthrie had passed through on his way north, with a mob of 700 sheep and 150 head of cattle.

When Guthrie and his stock arrived at Castlepoint he created quite a stir. Local Maori had never seen these strange new animals in such impressive numbers. Even more importantly, and of more practical benefit as far as Mrs Guthrie would be concerned, as a gesture of welcome and goodwill they agreed to charge a reasonable rate to erect a small raupo-thatched homestead for Guthrie's family.

Guthrie returned to Wellington, where his wife and family were waiting, only to hear the sad news of one of his daughters' death; but within a year the family sailed to Castlepoint, and finally rowed ashore at Deliverance Cove to become Castlepoint's first founding family. The sheep and cattle Guthrie had sent ahead had flourished in his absence, quickly forming herds to graze among the fern, flax, toetoe and scrubby manuka on the hills surrounding the bay. Local Maori described how 'five chiefs before' (some time in the 1600s), the whole area had been covered in dense native forest, which was destroyed in a massive bushfire. Evidence to back up their story was found in abundance once ploughs began to turn the soil, turning up old matai, totara and maire roots and burned timber.

The stout-hearted settler Thomas Guthrie, founding father of Castlepoint. *Wairarapa Archive*

The Guthries' first year on the station, 1848, would prove to be a hard one. Among other things, as if the backbreaking physical work and social isolation weren't enough, a strong earthquake shattered their chimney. But people who journey to the end of the earth aren't generally those who give up easily, and soon the Guthries, along with the other Pakeha sheep farmers in the Wairarapa, were providing a steady wool clip from their Spanish merino sheep, competing favourably for quality with New South Wales, the other major supplier at the time.

But, as they say, everything comes at a price. As well as providing a good wool clip, during wet winters the merinos were prone to infestations of footrot and scab — the latter being treated by dipping in an infusion of boiled tobacco water and arsenic, infamous for taking a toll on the dippers as well as the dipped. Fortunately, Guthrie was able to avoid the wholesale destruction of his flock, and the resulting bankruptcy, which saw many of his contemporaries go under.

Despite the exhausting effort Guthrie was devoting to the fledgling station, technically his land deal was questionable. A year before he had made his arrangement, the Native Land Purchase Ordnance of 1846 made purchase of land and occupation under native lease arrangements illegal. Like many of his Pakeha contemporaries, who were desperate to buy the land they had been told was there for the taking, Guthrie chose to ignore this inconvenient fact and continued on regardless. In 1853, Land Purchase Commissioner Donald McLean bought up 1,700,000 acres in the Wairarapa, for £13,000; and one of the first deals to be concluded within this massive total was the Castlepoint Block, from the Whareama River in the south to the Waimate Stream in the north. Witnesses to the purchase, which was agreed at a sum of £2500, were Thomas Guthrie, his children's new tutor William Marshall and John Sutherland, a stock-holder at Mataikona. Land was set aside for local Maori at both Whakataki and Castlepoint. Finally, Guthrie had been able to legally purchase the land he had already settled and broken in, although only with the financial assistance of English millionaire and investor Algernon Tollemache, who had his economic fingers in similar pies all along the East Coast.

Sea Transport

Not long after establishing Castlepoint Station, Guthrie had bought a small cutter, the *Kitty Clover,* which he used to pick up vital supplies from Wellington. During the 1850s the *Kitty,* as she was generally known, had become the chief supply vessel for the district, earning Guthrie the additional role of harbourmaster — not that he needed the extra work. Deliverance Cove was the landing place for many East Coast settlers, including the Holes family, who settled at Okau, near Whakataki. Their arrival was typical and is aptly described by John Holes:

> *There was a heavy north-easterly sea running and the* Esther *could not get into the bay. Three families were placed in a small rowboat, but there were only one or two who knew anything about pulling. We were soon all drenched to the skin and three of us were engaged in bailing out the water, two of us with our boots. There were two fat sheep on board and we had an argument about chucking them overboard to lighten the boat. The owners of the sheep would not agree, as these animals were especially valuable in those days. Old Tom Guthrie saw what was happening and came out through the Gap in the* Kitty Clover. *He managed to pick us up and returned with us through the Gap. Fortunately everything was saved, including the sheep.*

Castlepoint was isolated from other settlements further inland, but remained connected to the rest of the country by virtue of its natural harbour.

There were other challenges to keep life interesting — the following year a worker drowned trying to rescue a cattlebeast that had broken away and swum out onto the reef.

Steamers gradually began to replace the sailing ships, and by 1860 were prevalent, making the loading of wool and other commodities much easier. They anchored offshore and surfboats would ferry goods both ways. Typically, the steamer would anchor in the bay, then signal favourable conditions with a loud blast of the ship's horn. This would be the signal for station-holders to gather at the beach to collect their consignments, although some would already have been camped out for some time. Most orders were by the ton, and were usually deposited on the beach above the high-water mark. But if the station-holders were delayed, or the tide was running unusually high, it wasn't unknown for bales of perishable goods, such as flour and sugar, to be ruined by the incoming tide — a costly, and often belt-tightening, lesson.

The steamers were efficient, but they weren't always plain-sailing. On 4 October 1860 Robert Langdon, of Whareama, was there to watch the arrival of the steamer *White Swan*, and witnessed the following:

She came in sight and all hands got ready to go off to her. She was to take on board 450 sheep for Mr Guthrie. The boat was launched and five hands got into her, Charlie the Swede, Morrison, Tom Hales and Mr Groves, Mr Guthrie steering. They got through the breakers and were, we thought, quite safe, when a heavy sea struck her and she capsized. All hands were saved with difficulty, but the steamer did not wait but immediately went on for her destination leaving her freight and passengers behind.

One can imagine the curses called down upon the heads of those on the *White Swan*, and perhaps some of them stuck, as two years later she left Napier with sixty passengers only to strike a reef off Uriti Point, where she sank. Fortunately, all aboard made it safely to shore in lifeboats.

Descendants of early settlers re-enact a settler landing in the bay at Castlepoint, met by a bullock-wagon. *John Broad collection*

By 1865 Guthrie had been working Castlepoint's original 30,000 acres for more than seventeen hard years, and at fifty was no longer a young man, as they counted such things in those days. In that time the station had become a significant investment, and after selling the 10,000-acre southern block to the Reverend JC Andrew, Guthrie and his financial partner Tollemache put up the remaining 20,000 acres for sale.

An inventory of the station's assets at that time lists a homestead, woolshed, a number of staff houses and outbuildings, the thriving hotel and an attached eleven-room dwelling, a store, a wool store and stables, a blacksmith's shop and a boatshed, as well as a dairy, bakehouse, fowlhouse and butcher's shop.

It wasn't a good time to be selling — further north the New Zealand wars between Maori and Pakeha had escalated and while the Hauhau movement had been suppressed in the Wairarapa, it was still going strong in the Hawke's Bay. News had filtered south of Te Kooti's massacre of settlers in Poverty Bay and investors were cautious. The Castle Point Rifle Volunteers had formed in 1863,

with Guthrie as captain; in 1866 they were reorganized as a cavalry unit. While they were called to active service in 1868, nothing further was required of them and by 1869 they were disbanded. Peace nestled down again over the hills and beaches of Castlepoint as the district and the station continued to grow, and lives went on with the seasons.

CASTLEPOINT CEMETERY

IN MEMORY OF

THE EARLY SETTLERS & THEIR FAMILYS BURIED HERE

JOHN BUXTON	THOS GUTHRIE Jnr.
HENRY BUXTON	Mrs KENWICK
JAMES BENNETT	WILLIAM LOCKHART
EDWIN H. BURLING	SAMUEL JOHNSON
CAPTAIN CROUCHER	SAMUEL MADDEN
JOHN DUNN	LIZZIE LIVERTON
BESSIE GREENLAND	J.H. SAVAGE
JAMES GRAHAM	CHARLES SEAGER
SELINA GROVES	J. OSBORNE
WILLIAM GROVES	J. RICHARDSON
Mrs T. HALES	J. THEOBOLD
THOS GUTHERIE Snr.	J. WHISHAW

LYDIA POTANGAROA
(LOST HER LIFE TRYING TO SAVE OTHERS)

In 1873 Castlepoint Station was finally sold, to the outgoing Premier of New Zealand and South Australia George Marsden Waterhouse, no less, who had already purchased the 20,000-acre Hungarua Station in the Wairarapa and 2000 acres of the historic Wharekaka block. For the grand sum of £15,000, Waterhouse's purchase included 9700 sheep and 200 head of cattle, with over 12,000 acres of freehold land, another 5000 acres leased from the government and a further 6000 acres still on lease from local Maori.

By this time Guthrie was fifty-eight, and the one-time dairyman had long since earned the respectful title of Father of the District. His wife, Ann, was revered up and down the coast for her practical knowledge and willingness to dispense aid for all sorts of ailments, and was in no small way responsible for the excellent relationship the Guthries enjoyed with local Maori. Their children had grown up fluent in the language, and Maori children in the district became fluent in English in return.

Thomas wasn't cut out for retirement, and within a year the old settler had died. He was buried at Castlepoint beside his son, Thomas Guthrie Junior, who at just twenty-four years of age had died before him, drowned in the Whakataki River. Father and son lie in a small settlers' cemetery at Castlepoint, raised above the sealed road that now runs down to the water and the carefully clipped and tended seafront, neat as a pin in the summer sunshine. Ann Guthrie survived her husband by another five years, dying in 1879 at the age of sixty-three, and is buried at Porangahau, north of Castlepoint.

A black-and-white wooden sign at the Castlepoint cemetery records the names of the Guthries and one of Thomas Senior's daughters, Jane Whishaw, who died in 1871, along with twenty-four of their neighbours, including one Lydia Potangaroa, who 'lost her life trying to save others'. They all lie together beneath the quiet gravel, surrounded by low-growing pohutukawa. Each grave has its own story, but perhaps the most poignant of all lies with a grave over in the left-hand corner, fenced off from the others. Edwin Henry Burling 'met his death by his horse falling on him' on 12 May 1843, when he was just fourteen.

The sign is necessary, as not all the gravestones have survived intact and some of the graves are marked by stones whose details have weathered away — although the rock remains, an apt metaphor for life at Castlepoint, where the weather rules the land, and the people. It's a peaceful place to lie, especially when the sea is quiet, its constant roar and hiss ever-present, although soon dropping away into the background. Somehow it seems very fitting that the man who began the story of farming here, and two of his children, have joined their bones with the land to become a part of the enduring legacy of Castlepoint.

Opposite page: Castlepoint cemetery and the names of early settlers, Jetty Road, Castlepoint.

Deliverance Cove, otherwise known as 'The Gap', landing place of William Colenso and William Williams, the first Europeans to set foot on the shores of Castlepoint.

An age-old pastime beneath the lighthouse.

The landed gentry

As the colony became a country, inevitably the balance of power shifted. The pioneering men and women of the land were followed by financiers, politicians and men of substance. What began as one man's effort to provide a home for his family became a small part of another man's investment portfolio, which was then destined to become a portion of a rich man's estate. For the following 123 years, Castlepoint Station would be a family station in name only, as a series of managers would run it for a board of trustees.

Previous page:
The 'holiday
light', Castle Point
Lighthouse in
1930 beside its
oil store-houses.
Wairarapa Archive

THE HONOURABLE GEORGE WATERHOUSE didn't hold on to Castlepoint Station
for very long, and by 1876 it had been sold again, to yet another Honourable
from Wellington — Walter Woods Johnston.

Like Waterhouse, Johnston was a politician. He was the Member for
Manawatu in the House of Representatives, and the son of John Johnston,
founder of prominent coastal shipping firm Johnston and Co. There's
considerable irony in the fact that the money to buy Castlepoint came from a
family with close involvement in the now lucrative wool trade, a trade almost
entirely due to the earlier efforts of humbler men like Thomas Guthrie. While
farm labourers and men of the soil had broken in the land to make homes for
their families, the stations they created now became part of the investment
portfolios of much wealthier 'men of substance', as they would have been
described at the time.

Walter and
Cecilia Johnston,
purchasers of
Castlepoint Station
in 1876, one of
Walter's many
investments — 'a
man of substance'.
Wairarapa Archive

Walter Johnston was just such a man. Five years earlier he had married
Miss Cecilia Augusta Goring of Palmerston North, who came to the marriage from
Highden, an imposing rimu manor house with no fewer than fourteen bedrooms.
Already a very wealthy man, for Johnston Castlepoint was just one of his many
investments, as he forged ahead in business and politics, building his father's
company into a major player with branches throughout the North Island. Johnston
and Co. made excellent profits by exporting wool, flax, frozen and preserved meat
and other agricultural produce, and importing manufactured goods in return.

Johnston's first manager at Castlepoint was Harry Holmes, about whom not much is known. He was followed by Alan Cameron, a Boer War veteran with the New Zealand Expeditionary Force. While Cameron and his wife both made a significant contribution to the growing Castlepoint community, he was known to drink to excess, even by the standards of the day. It could be speculated that this was a response to his war experiences, from which he never fully recovered. Sadly, his inner demons finally got the better of him when he committed suicide at the Prince of Wales Hotel in Masterton. His final drink was a lethal dose of arsenic.

When Walter Johnston died in 1907, his widow, by now the mother of his seven children, enjoyed the benefits of a very substantial estate in the region of half a million pounds, a huge amount for the time, and she took sole charge of Castlepoint Station. When Cecilia Johnston came to visit, it was as a very wealthy

Cecilia Johnston and her four daughters, future heirs of Castlepoint Station.
Wairarapa Archive

woman with an entourage — on one occasion this included one of her four daughters, two grandchildren, two cousins, a car and chauffeur, two manservants, her personal maid, a dog and four parrots. Clearly, she was no Greta Garbo.

An extraordinary photograph shows a very correctly attired and bowler-hatted Cecilia seated sidesaddle on her horse, followed by a line of all four daughters, similarly dressed (above). If it wasn't for the distinctly colonial farm buildings and the gum trees in the background, you'd be forgiven for thinking they were five very proper Englishwomen about to take part in a Home Counties hunt.

Cecilia died in 1922, leaving Castlepoint to her four daughters, all of whom had married: Jane Turnbull, Ella Pharazyn, Sydney Holmes and Ida Mary Baldwin. The rest of the vast estate was divided among her three sons. Through the daughters, the Johnston family would retain control of Castlepoint for the next 122 years, during which time it would be run by a series of stewards and managers. They would continue the work Thomas Guthrie had begun and further break in the land, as farming became firmly entrenched as the economic engine driving the development of coastal Wairarapa.

The first manager employed by the Johnston daughters was Harold Scales, who guided the station through the Great Depression. Not much is known now about his farming methods, and Harold is best remembered for one of his horses, the renowned jumper 'Clinker'. A big, heavy, handsome horse who galloped like a thoroughbred, Clinker was famously able to clear the stock-yard rails, so it's not surprising that he and Harold cleaned up the prizes at horse shows up and down the country.

While the world was gripped by the Depression, this era sowed the seeds of New Zealand's prosperity, and was the prelude to the golden period when sheep farmers began to make serious money and were well on their way to becoming the single most important contributor to our national wealth. It's a well-worn phrase, but it's accurate — our prosperity as a nation came on the backs of our sheep. The wool and meat they produced fed and clothed the Empire, and the industry's economic significance can be seen in the fact that from 1916, the Crown controlled the buying and selling of the national wool clip.

By the turn of the century, most of the East Coast stations, including Castlepoint, had replaced their merino flocks with Lincolns. While the hardy merinos had been invaluable in breaking in rough country, once pastures had been established, the Lincoln yielded a heavier fleece. In time, the wool from Wairarapa's East Coast stations would be considered to be some of the best in the world.

The establishment of freezing works saw a demand for lighter carcasses, and eventually the Lincolns were themselves replaced, this time with Romneys, and sheep farming was set to flourish well into the twentieth century. Not a bad result, really: from 700 sheep in 1848 to world-class status in fewer than a hundred years.

It could be said that this mirrored the way the people changed, too. The tougher breeds, able to handle the rough conditions, came first and did the hard yards, to be followed in time, and usurped, by the more refined and economically astute.

Opposite page, top:
A Sunday outing,
Castlepoint reef
in 1900.
Wairarapa Archive

Bottom: The
Castlepoint stock
yards in 1922.
Laing family collection

The Castle Point Lighthouse

The new logo for Castlepoint Station features one of the area's most recognizable landmarks, the Castle Point Lighthouse. The lighthouse has been there since 1913, when it became the last manned lighthouse to be established in this country, and it's still the first sign of New Zealand for ships approaching from the eastern seaboard, sitting as it does on a high point of the reef, to the north of Castle Rock.

The iron tower was cast in Wellington by Luke & Sons Foundry and shipped up the coast by barge. It is constructed of seven rings, each of which is 3 metres high, and standing at 51.8 metres above sea level it remains one of the tallest in the Lighthouse Service, although it is no longer manned.

The first light was an incandescent oil-burning lamp, and in 1961 the lighthouse was connected to mains electricity. Now using a single 1000 watt incandescent bulb, its light is magnified out to 26 nautical miles, flashing three times every 3 seconds.

Originally, the light was rotated by a weight, and Castle Point was the second lighthouse in New Zealand to utilize a mercury-filled bath as a base to ensure an even rotation. The Wairarapa earthquakes of 1942, one of which was of magnitude 7.6 and felt as far away as Dunedin, soon put paid to that, with the principal keeper at the time describing how a quake at 8.15 p.m. sent the mercury spilling out of the apparatus bowl, all over the machine and the lighthouse floor, instantly stopping the light. He managed to clean it up and get the light operating again after 45 minutes, but at 11.18 p.m. there was another huge jolt, which smashed the bowl and sent mercury pouring out, again stopping the light. Fortunately, that saw the end of the mercury flotation system; it made life a lot less dangerous for the keepers but much less interesting for visiting children, who used to be given a drop of mercury in a matchbox to play with, to their endless fascination.

Castle Point started out as a three-man lighthouse station, later reduced to two, and by the mid 'seventies there was a single keeper and his family. In 1922 one of the keepers at the time fell some 6 metres to his death while re-fixing telephone wires blown loose by the capricious wind; his ghost was said to occupy one of the keepers' houses for many years afterwards.

Unpredictable seas have swept many fishermen to their deaths off the reef below the lighthouse, adding to the stress for keepers during the busy holiday months. While the lighthouse was out of the danger zone and well-secured, the steep track up to it from the beach wasn't always quite so safe. A change of shift at night meant climbing up a steep, narrow track with a storm lantern; on one occasion, a heavy southerly gale came right over the track, washing away part of it and the handrail. The keeper on roster to relieve at midnight only managed to reach the lighthouse with great difficulty, and was blown off the bridge and onto his back while trying to make his way to work. Not surprisingly, the keeper he was due to relieve decided to stay put until daybreak.

Back in the days when the lighthouse station was fully staffed, the principal keeper and his family lived in a purpose-built house overlooking the bay. There were also three other keepers' houses, an assortment of outbuildings, a vegetable garden and a paddock for dairy cows nestled in the area below. It was a popular posting as, unlike most other postings, this one was close to civilization, and the keepers and their families were quickly integrated into community life.

Automation of lighthouses began in this country in 1970, and while the last keeper, Grant Hinchliffe, was a bitter opponent of automation, he finished his posting at Castle Point on 31 August 1988, when the lighthouse was finally automated. After many years of faithful service, the keepers had been replaced by a computer link to Wellington.

A black-backed gull soaring high above Castlepoint near its nesting ground on Castle Rock.

The interior workings of the lighthouse, including a kerosene vaporizer, pulley and cogs, all now defunct. The lighthouse is powered by electricity and monitored remotely by a central computer in Wellington.

In 1928, management of Castlepoint Station passed on to a newlywed couple, Ferdinand (Fer) and Peggy Ashworth, who took over a large staff mostly of men. The roster included shepherds, cadets, fencers, rabbiters, gorse-grubbers, a cowman/gardener and the one person no station could run without — the cook.

A typical shepherd's wage in the 1930s was £2 a week, and for young men who worked at Castlepoint, it was a relatively isolated life. Time off consisted of plenty of card games, with crib and 500 being perennial favourites, and in common with the rest of the country, there was rugby on Saturdays.

Although cars had become more commonplace as the roads and the economy improved, going to Masterton was still a bit of a trek. Without electricity, all cooking was done on coal ranges, which were also equipped with wetbacks to provide hot water, and lighting had progressed from candles to kerosene lanterns.

While the Ashworths would remain at Castlepoint for the next two decades, Fer's stewardship was never easy. In his time there, Castlepoint survived drought, the Great Depression and World War II. The war brought a dramatic drop in the price for wool, a major component of the station's income, when fixed prices were introduced as a wartime regulation. Not surprisingly, like others before him, Fer began to rely on the drink, becoming a regular at the Whakataki Pub. He was usually in a hurry to get there, and had a series of small horse-gates cut into the fences on the station so that he could make it back before he was missed every lunchtime.

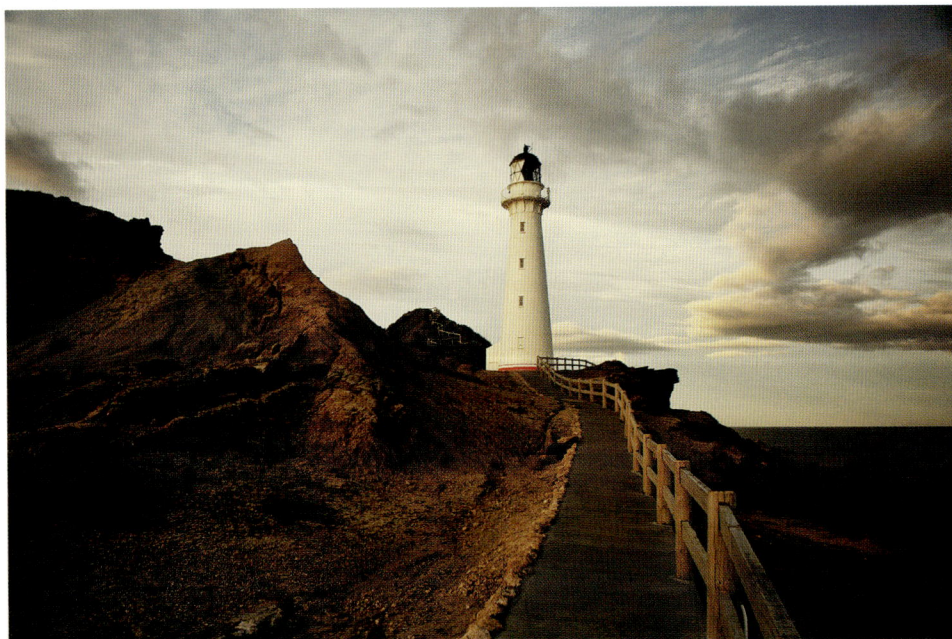

The narrow and windswept track to the lighthouse, an everyday passage of duty for lighthouse keepers in the days of manned lighthouses.

If life was tough for the adults, for their children, growing up at Castlepoint was anything but, as recounted here by Penny Ashworth:

Summers were glorious and seemed to be filled endlessly with sun, tennis and swimming. There always seemed to be people staying, friends and relatives either with us or renting baches. Then in the evenings we would always have charades and parlour games. Singing around the piano was a favourite too. Despite the seemingly casual way of life, a certain standard of dress was apparent and it was always white for tennis. Every afternoon the men put on their long cream flannels and of course changed for dinner every night. It gave it all a structure of formality totally acceptable for the times. We had picnics at the foot of Castle Rock on sundial time (Father drew sundials in the sand as no watches were taken).

The seasons were defined by the farming activities of lambing, docking, mustering, shearing and dipping. So exciting were the chances to go inside the lighthouse, the walks around the high top of the reef, learning to swim in the Basin, climbing over the rocks to the cave at the foot of the lighthouse headland, fishing for herrings and cod from the same rocks.

Beside the dairy at the back of the homestead was a storeroom that was always locked. I remember the excitement of going in with Mother as there were huge crates of sultanas, dates, sacks of sugar, porridge and flour. It was set up like a shop with jars of Marmite, packets of baking powder and cornflour.

There were hens too, which used to run free amongst the walnut trees in the orchard but were later rounded up and controlled by a definite henhouse with its own run by the vegetable garden. When they were running wild we would be sent to find the nests and there was great excitement when you came across one, perhaps at the heart of a toetoe bush.

We had a dressmaker who stayed for a week twice yearly in autumn and spring to make the forthcoming season's clothes, and if Mother was ever away we would go to the cookhouse for dinner with our father for overcooked roasts, the silverbeet boiling all afternoon, black by the time it was served but tasting delicious suffused with the thickest brown gravy.

So many memories and an underlying knowledge that for us, as children, we were blessed to have had such a sheltered, secure childhood growing up in the environment of Castlepoint.

The majestic Castle Point Lighthouse before the
sun rising in the east.

When the Ashworths retired in 1948, Stewart Harvey took over as manager, arriving alone in the middle of August. His wife, Noni, had decided to wait out the winter, and arrived in November with their three children: Robin, Brian and Bruce, their new baby.

A sample of Harvey's diary entries from November 1951 through to September 1952 paints a vivid picture of life at Castlepoint in the early 'fifties.

Nov 15th: A tragedy on reef about 4.30. A man from Masterton was drowned. He fell off High Top. Attempts to rescue failed.

Nov 17th: Took a ride along the beach as far as Okau to see if any sign of missing body, but nothing to be seen.

Nov 30th: Fine and warm but blowing howling north west. The ground is getting hard on top but country still green which is very unusual for this time of the year.

Dec 16th: Connelly the cook is on the booze. He made a fine job of it this time. Can't see him being right for work tomorrow. The men had to get their own meals. Old John the gardener is back at work which is a real surprise.

Feb 1st: Blowing a gale from nor-west. The yards were terrible to work in with dust.

Feb 2nd: We have had about 10 days of gale force nor-westers — very drying, but the crops have stood up to it remarkably well.

Feb 23rd: Am having trouble with the Cook and Broughton. Putting the cook off on Monday. The hardest task is finding another ...

Apr 26th: Strong nor-west wind. Went up to Mataikona to inspect new hut that is being erected. Road was in a shocking state. Pulled Mr Morgan's car through for him, after it had become stuck last night.

May 8th: Bitten by a katipo spider. Very painful. Taken into Dr — having penicillin injections. The missing launch Southern Cross turned up at 11.50am today after having been missing a week in high seas. The crew were exhausted and came ashore. They are fortunate to be alive. Peter Laing came out to start as head shepherd.

July 10th: Day very cold and wet. One of the roughest days since I have been at Castlepoint. Snow on the hills.

Sept 29th: A very heavy quake in afternoon but no damage.

It wouldn't be the last time Peter Laing's name would appear in connection with Castlepoint, by any means; when Stewart Harvey retired later in 1952, his successor — Peter — was already in place. He'd be there for the next thirty-nine years.

The Laing years

They called him the Master, and for many years he ruled with a rod of iron. Peter Laing left his mark on the station, and on the local community. The penultimate station manager, he was an innovator and a hard worker, who expected nothing less than total dedication from those around him, including his own family. Providing an invaluable link to the past for the current owners, Peter Laing will long be remembered for his years of dedication and strength — a true man of the land.

PETER LAING FIRST CAME TO CASTLEPOINT STATION as a shepherd in 1948, returning later as head shepherd, and eventually taking over as manager in 1955, when Stu Harvey retired. He wouldn't leave until his retirement in 1991, making his tenure the longest to date — even longer than that of Thomas Guthrie, who started it all. Not surprisingly, Laing left his mark on the place, and the memory of one of the district's notable identities remains strong today.

When he installed his young wife, Nan, and their three children, Bill, Fiona (Fe) and Trish, in the farmhouse, the station was already a small, tight-knit community, with a permanent population living in a dozen households. There were the drivers — tractor driver Rodger Hawthorn, truck driver Gordon Meikle and bus driver Dick McIsaac; a fencer, John Murison; the carpenter and his wife, Bert and Molly Culver; Blue Tyakke and his wife — he was the gardener and she was the cook; two cadet shepherds and a cowman/shepherd; storekeeper Frank Crop; Bill Wooding, an agar collector and general handyman; fishermen Les Brown, Wally Zander, and Harry Emerson and his wife Doris; lighthouse keepers Ken Armstrong and Ray Bateman; the Dellabarcas and the McFederies, who were seasonal fishermen; plus the schoolteacher.

Of course the names would change over the years, as people came and went, in the nature of a big station, but the jobs remained pretty much the same, and throughout it all Peter and Nan Laing provided the steady hands that kept it all ticking over, managing the Johnston family's investment through some tough and testing years. That Peter Laing was a worker, and a tough man, was legend. That he was also rock-solid, hard-line, strong-willed and totally devoted to Castlepoint Station was accepted without a doubt. He had to be, to hold together a whole community. It took mana, something Peter Laing had in spades, as his good friend Roddy McKenzie recalled:

Opposite page,
top: Peter Laing
in the stables at
Castlepoint.
Laing family collection

Bottom: Light-
house keeper
Ken Armstrong.
Wairarapa Archive

> *Peter was a big man, but never the one in a suit, and he certainly stood out above everyone else, always the person people would ask about. He was also very much a people's person and would only have to begin talking to someone and immediately they were friends. But he wasn't afraid to tell you what he thought. You would go to a meeting out at Tinui and he would always make his presence felt. He stood over you — and always with that hat on!*

Together with Nan, Peter would bring Castlepoint well and truly into the twentieth century, turning it into a highly productive, modern coastal hill-country station. The productivity gains he was able to achieve would earn him widespread respect from other farmers, who understood the hard yakka and devotion that

went into those impressive figures. He was particularly good at breaking in back country and became renowned for his early adoption of cutting-edge pastoral techniques and a fresh approach to stock rotation that paid handsome dividends for the Johnston family shareholders.

During the station's heyday, from the 'fifties to the 'eighties, scores of young shepherds and cadets came to Castlepoint to learn from 'the Master'. They were the good years, when sheer hard work and dedication saw its just reward as prices soared and New Zealand's agricultural export markets continued to expand.

One of Peter Laing's deeply held beliefs was that everything should earn its keep, not least his children, who all have fond memories of growing up at Castlepoint and the sterling work ethic their father instilled. His daughter Trish remembers working for her father for three or four years, as a land girl, with her own team of six dogs 'and my trusty horse, Prince'. She described her father as very hard but fair, and said she was treated pretty much the same as all the boys. Like them, she remembers her dad's way of taking them out to do 'a quick job' that usually ended up being just one of a whole *list* of quick jobs, or was on a part of the farm that took half a day to get to — and inevitably ended up taking most of the day to complete. 'In the long run you came out as a stronger person.'

Opposite page, top: Peter Laing mustering sheep at Ngakawau Beach. *Laing family collection*

Bottom: Castlepoint Station staff with the Johnny Walker shearing gang and Nan Laing, seated front row, second from right. *Laing family collection*

Until recently, Prince was still there, superannuated and pretty much toothless, living out the last of his days in the house paddock, where he supervised the other thirteen horses. People would call out 'gidday' to him when he was by the fence, and he accepted it as his rightful due.

The Laing's eldest daughter, Fe, has similar memories of hard work.

We were the after-hours staff and official gate-openers. Gate-opening for Dad was an art as he never stopped the Land Rover from moving forward, so you had to leap out and run to the gate, undo the latch and swing it open, all the while the vehicle was getting closer. Then as it came through you would quickly fasten it otherwise you had to run halfway down the paddock to catch up!

To this day I still rush to open gates … We were certainly cut no slack. When it came to jobs like fencing, if a post or strainer had to go down the line and we were handy you were expected to take it there. There was no doubt that Dad worked everybody hard, but he was always there, working just as hard. The work ethic that he instilled in the staff stood them in good stead for their farming careers. Many complained at the long hours, but they forgot that while they were over in the pub enjoying a cold beer, Dad was either still out checking stock or in the office sorting the following week's programme.

They still have lots of gates on the station, and surely every variation of gate fastening known to man. Jim Wood, Emily Crofoot's father, is convinced that Kiwi farmers lie awake at night dreaming up new ways of fastening a gate, and some of those who are doing the job now would have been from Peter Laing's time, for sure. Nothing gets wasted on a truly productive farm.

Castlepoint under Peter Laing had a reputation for long hours, with station-hands sometimes working up to 120 hours per week — and the station used every minute. Bruce Skeet, a shepherd in the 1960s, recalls those days:

> *Peter was a hell of a good boss. He was fair but extremely hard. We would have four o'clock mornings for 20 days in a row. And if you had a night on the booze it would make no difference. Time and time again we'd be at a party and realize there was only an hour left before work, so we'd scream back to the station, throw off our dinner suits, saddle up the horses and away we'd go for the day. Useless as tits on a bull but that's the way it was. There would be times when you'd fall asleep on your horse. On one occasion the boys didn't even get changed from the night before.*

The longer staff worked on the station, the more they realized that Peter Laing's reputation was well earned. But then he had to be a hard taskmaster, to tame the huge economic engine that Castlepoint had become, and manage the strange mix of characters and personalities that came and went for forty years, melding them into a vibrant, functioning community that 'earned its keep'. Peter Laing oversaw years of scrub-cutting, and fought a perennial battle with gorse and scrubby manuka, which had spread wildly after the settlers burned out the competition.

This strong man, one of thirteen children and a quintessential 'good Kiwi joker', in the vernacular of the time, also had his soft side, exemplified by his long and successful marriage to his soul mate, Nancy Jackson, known and loved universally as 'Nan'. One of the great identities of Castlepoint, she was its welcoming heart and at the centre of the station's life for many years. A warm and friendly woman, accepting all the diverse and sometimes eccentric personalities who washed up there over the years, Nan was Peter's calm centre.

Her good friend Elaine Foreman knew Nan from her early twenties. The pretty young schoolteacher had already met and married Peter in 1953, when he was head shepherd, and the young couple had just moved from the head shepherd's cottage to live in the station homestead.

They were both very young, and it must have been a monumental task for a young couple to undertake. But each of them in their own way became the very heart of that station ...

Nan extended her definition of family to anyone else who worked on the station and lived in the community, from the alcoholic cowmen/gardeners through station cooks, casual workers and the youngest of novice shepherds to the newly married wives of head shepherds, schoolteachers, lighthouse keepers and their families — all were regarded as part of one big family.

ELAINE FOREMAN

That Nan was also a hard worker goes without saying. With no electricity at the station until 1959, there were none of the labour-saving devices housewives in urban New Zealand were already taking for granted. While the farmhouse floor-plan still had a 'maids room', the maids had disappeared long ago; it also listed something called a 'lamp room', where each day lamp glasses were washed, wicks trimmed and lamps refilled with either kerosene or white spirits.

In the days before electricity, if you needed hot water in a hurry and the coal range wasn't fired up, it often meant lighting a contraption called a Primus, a portable pressurized kerosene stove. At Castlepoint one stood in the kitchen, ready for use. Lighting it involved pouring methylated spirits around the burner, then lighting the meths with a match to preheat (prime) the kerosene tank, which would then be given a couple of pumps. By the time the meths had burned out, the kerosene was warm enough to start flowing out through the jets and the Primus would be ready to be lit.

I remember one early morning when I went down to the kitchen to heat up the baby's bottle. I must have over-primed the Primus. Ignited kerosene squirted all over the kitchen curtains and set them ablaze. I ran screaming down the hall and woke Peter. He took a flying leap on to the bench and grabbed the remains of the flaming curtains to douse them in the sink. But he hadn't accounted for the plastic-coated stretchy wire threaded through the top, which was red hot! The skin on his hands just peeled, a real mess ...

NAN LAING

It was no wonder so many of New Zealand's original farmhouses went up in smoke. Like Castlepoint's homestead, many of them were isolated, built of timber, lit with candles and kerosene lamps, and had wood and coal ranges for cooking and heating, and fireplaces in the bedrooms. Another close call for the old farmhouse came when Nan Laing acquired the latest iron on the market — another pump-action contraption, with a tank filled with white spirit. After giving it a couple of good, hard pumps, she put a match to the jets and was horrified to see it go up in a ball of flames. Luckily, she was better prepared this time and, using the hearth shovel, scooped it up and hurled it out the window, where it remained — best place for any iron, some would say.

Before 1959, Nan's wash-house boasted a copper in the corner, then a couple of concrete tubs and a hand-wringer set up between the two. Wash day began by stoking the fire beneath the copper with anything that would burn — pine cones, kindling, firewood. Once the water was hot, towels, sheets and anything else able to withstand the copper was first boiled, then fished out with a strong stick and dumped into a tub of cold water for their first rinse. Anything else was soaked, laid out on the corrugated wooden washboard, then given a good scrubbing by hand with pale-yellow Sunlight soap. Everything was wrung out through the hand-wringer into the second tub, before being rinsed again, this time with the addition of a Reckitt's 'blue bag', a mysterious little parcel of deepest blue that was supposed to make the whites whiter; it was also the accepted treatment for a bee-sting back in those days.

And after this back-breaking effort, the washing still had to be hung out on the clothes-line in the hope it would dry enough to be brought in before it rained. It was hot and steamy work in summer, with the copper boiling and the fire roaring, and in those days wash day meant pretty much all day.

With no handy supermarket to stock up from, Nan was expected to keep the station supplied and able to feed all hands, and that meant making the most of the fruit and vegetables grown on the property, with nothing going to waste. In those days, this entailed mammoth bottling and preserving sessions, with preserving pans bubbling and bottles in the coal oven sterilizing, as a mountain of fresh produce became neatly stacked rows of up to 300 preserving jars. Nan bottled fruit from the farm's own orchard and made homemade spaghetti that no Italian would recognize but which every child of the 'fifties would, along with tomato relish, sauces and jams.

Preserving also involved meat. With no electricity to run freezers, they ate a lot of pickled meat, which at the time was the standard way of preserving it. Corned beef and silverside, or pickled pork, are the modern supermarket equivalents, but in those days it was just pickled mutton and beef. At Castlepoint, they used a large concrete trough as their pickle barrel, filled with up to 40 gallons of water, salt and saltpetre, which made up the brine used to preserve the meat. The trick lay in making sure the brine was salty enough, and the usual way of testing this was to throw in a potato — if the potato floated, the brine was ready. In later years Nan Laing would recall how difficult it was to keep the pickling trough clean; although, to her credit, no one died of food poisoning!

Eggs were kept for when the chooks weren't laying using Norton's Egg Preserver. Eggs were placed in a mixture made from the preservative and water. They would keep for up to a year and only needed to be rinsed before using. Some people rubbed their eggs with Ovalene, another product, which made the eggs slippery.

During the early 'fifties the station began to employ married cooks, with the husband usually delegated to look after the cows, vege garden, fowls and pigs while his wife cooked and prepared all the meals for the staff. This included an early morning tea, cooked breakfast, smoko, lunch, and dinner in the evening.

A typical breakfast might be porridge, chops, bacon or sausages and eggs, sometimes some bubble and squeak — refried leftover vegetables from the night before — plus

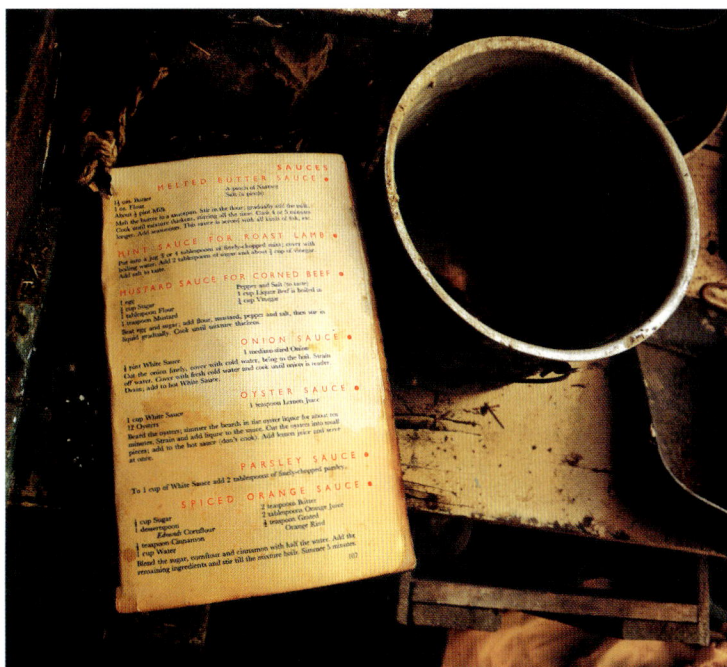

Cook's kitchen at the shepherds' Ngakawau whare, otherwise known as the 'Ngakawau Hotel'.

toast and marmalade. Every cook worth her salt knew that working men needed a substantial breakfast to set them up, and especially so when work meant a gruelling day following Peter's tough no-holds-barred schedule.

The low wages of the time reflected the fact that staff on the coast in those days were all employed 'fully found', which meant that the station provided them with food, power, accommodation and telephone. This in turn meant that Nan and the cook had to make sure there was always enough on hand to feed everybody. As a result, the store orders, which initially came up from Johnston and Co. General Merchants in Wellington twice a year, were enormous. The masses of food, enough to cater for up to sixteen to eighteen staff plus casual workers for six months, would travel up by rail and be collected by the station truck, and then would be stacked away carefully in a separate storehouse known as the pataka.

In the Pataka

There would be cases of dried fruit, huge tea chests, sacks of soap powder, rice, rolled oats, flour, sugar, large tins of baking powder, 5lb tins of assorted jams, large kilo jars of peanut butter and Marmite, drums of cleaning materials and there would also be dozens of mouse traps on the list. It was always a huge task putting together a store order. By the end of six months, after sifting out the weevils from the flour, sorting through the shredded toilet rolls and luncheon wrap, it was always time for celebration as the new stores would again fill the shelves of the pataka. The old straw broom would come out, debris cleaned up, mouse traps reactivated and we would be ready and waiting for our new shipment. At least for a few months we would be relieved of having to pluck out offending foreign matter from our cooking ingredients, although Peter always used to say that a little extra protein never did anyone any harm ...
NAN LAING

The culture of preserving and making good use of whatever the land would produce was also running strongly on the other side of the world, as described in a *GCA Bulletin* published in July 1941, just a few years earlier. At Braewold, on the other side of the world, Emily Crofoot's grandmother, Mrs Hollingsworth Wood, was busy filling her root and vegetable cellar:

These include potatoes, beets, celery, chicory, turnips, pears, onions, parsnips, cabbages, salsify and carrots, the last keep until mid-June, as do apples. She always buys oranges in crates and stores them in the cellar to use at the family's convenience. Mrs Wood says there are three essentials in building a root cellar: good drainage, sufficient insulation and continual ventilation.

The floor of Mrs Wood's cellar has a base, first of coal cinders eight inches deep, then covered with concrete. This insures a durable floor, readily cleaned out after sand and earth used in storing the vegetables has been removed. The cellar was dug out of the side of a hill and lined with rock, then pointed up with cement. It is twenty feet long and eight feet high, with ventilation shafts covered by a wire mesh to keep out rats and mice. Inside the root cellar are wooden shelves wide enough for holding baskets. They run along one side only, to leave the rest of the space for forcing endive, blanching celery etc, and are high enough above the ground so that barrels can stand under them.

Opposite page, top: Past and present-day lamp-glasses at Castlepoint Station.

Bottom: The killing shed.

Nan Laing and Martha Wood would have understood each other perfectly.

When the shearing gangs moved in to Castlepoint, they brought with them their own cooks, who always had an off-sider to help them in the kitchen, especially when it came to preparing the main meal of the day. A sit-down dinner would be on the table promptly at 6 p.m., with shearing stopping on the dot of 5 p.m. and the gang having a beer together while they waited.

It was plain food but there was plenty of it. Each cook had his or her own speciality: one was famous for his mint sauce; he used to collect and dry great bunches of mint in season, then crumble the leaves between his hands, storing the dried mint in glass jars to be made into the best mint sauce this side of the black stump. Hungry men would expect to be served steaming plates of meat and vegetables. Some vegetables, like the infamous black silverbeet, would have been stewed for so long they were barely recognizable, but were always covered in thick, delicious brown gravy — if the cook was any good. In those days cooks stood or fell on the strength of their gravy.

On one occasion, the cook's off-sider was her husband, a particularly small and scrawny-looking individual. He nicked off to the pub — a crucial error of judgement — and was noticeably absent when the time came to dish up. The cook was not amused and everyone knew the little man was about to walk into a world of pain. He finally turned up, worse for wear. As she saw him staggering up from the car, the cook snapped. 'I'll give you a drink, you little bugger,' she yelled, then promptly whipped the top off a bottle of beer, got him into a headlock and rammed it down his throat. Those who watched in horrified fascination noted that she used the same technique you'd use to drench a cow. She didn't let go until the bottle was empty, by which time his nose and ears were well and truly frothing. Suffice to say, the little fella never snuck off again while he was at Castlepoint.

Despite the station being beside the sea, Castlepoint shepherds were known as mutton-munchers, usually having mutton for breakfast, lunch and dinner. It wasn't uncommon for cooks to serve chops and fried potatoes for breakfast, cold mutton and boiled potatoes for lunch and roast mutton and roast potatoes for dinner. All this meat and no handy butcher or freezer meant that the station needed its own killing house. Each Saturday, the shepherds would take their turn to kill up to six sheep, providing the cook and the station's dogs with fresh meat and dog tucker for the following week.

It was a gruesome but necessary part of station life, an exciting Saturday ritual for the young Trish Laing, who described it in some detail in the 2010 book *Castlepoint: coastal station and settlement*. The old killing shed still stands at

The former Castlepoint killing shed.

the station, although it's no longer used today, having been replaced by a new purpose-built one over by the dog kennels, with cattle now aged and processed off-site by a local butcher in Masterton.

Saturday morning we always spent at the killing shed. Mum would dress me in my waterproofs and bid me farewell for the morning. Myself and Cathy Priggen loved these days and would spend most of the time watching, waiting, ready for the kill. As the boys cut the throat they would try spraying us with the blood as it shot out the neck and we would retreat with an almighty scream. It was my job to strip all the intestines from the gut and get all the grass out. I took this job very seriously and prided myself on getting to the end of the intestine without a break. All the innards were then put in the boiler at the shed and cooked up as dog tucker. With all the blood being washed down the drain into the creek, the eels had a field day. Afterwards Johnny Walker from the shearing gang would pay us 20 cents for each eel we could catch!

July 1959 saw domestic life at the station change significantly. There had been talk of getting the power on for a decade, but Castlepoint had always been way down the list because of its isolation. Finally, the wait was over and, to speed things up, station-hands installed power poles from the corner of Tinui Valley Road all the way up to the station itself. Working in conjunction with the company contracted to lay on the power, Gordon Meikle and Henry Williams drove their tractor and truck tirelessly, carting poles and whatever else was needed. Wiring all the buildings on the property was an enormous task, and Nan, eight months pregnant at the time, found herself toiling over a hot coal range cooking for a team of electricians. It was exhausting and the job seemed endless, as poles and bales of wire were humped through the scrub and the electricians worked overtime to get it all done. Finally, after a bit of kidding around, the moment came, and Nan was asked to switch on the power.

We had light! The fridge started working, the stove started glowing, and the kettle started to boil — all our birthdays had come at once. We had a wonderful celebration that night — anyone would have thought we'd won the Art Union [the 'fifties equivalent of Lotto]. Bernie, one of Ted's electricians, had done a wonderful job. He also did a wonderful job of draining our liquor supply. Mind you, there were many others not too far behind.

Before we went to bed that night, we went round all the buildings and
turned on every light. We just couldn't believe the glow that met our gaze.
Light here, light there, lights inside, lights outside ... What a thrill that was.
Household tasks became much more pleasurable.
NAN LAING

The fact that Peter and Nan Laing stayed in the district after they retired and
were more than willing to help the new owners is a mark of their generosity of
spirit; and for the Crofoots, having Peter available for advice, as well as longtime
Castlepoint employee Gordon Meikle living just over the road, was invaluable.
As a result, the new owners have a deep appreciation of exactly what was achieved
during those momentous years in the 'fifties, 'sixties and 'seventies.

One of the greatest gifts Peter Laing left to future generations of Castlepoint
farmers is the amazing battle he fought with gorse, practically eradicating it from
the station, in a ceaseless war of attrition. According to the Crofoots' long-time
friend Donald Cooper, 'He sprayed it and sprayed it and sprayed it and there's
virtually none left — in fact I think gorse is pretty much held to the western
boundary now — and that's a hell of an achievement, because gorse is like
another mortgage.'

I knew Peter Laing because he'd retired here, and I used to work for a man
who'd been a junior to Peter and married one of his nieces. Where my wife Jill
and I farm in central Hawke's Bay there were people who'd been at Castlepoint,
so they knew it in the old days and I used to talk to them about it. He certainly
ruled there with an iron hand and he did it very successfully, but in a very
different environment. Peter would probably look and scratch his head at some
of the things that have been done since his day, but times have changed.

In his day he took Castlepoint from a pretty average place and he very
much made it — he ran it very well and he was quite progressive for his time,
with the amount of fertilizer he put in, and the way he maintained high stock
numbers under difficult conditions; in fact they were amazing, and a lot of
people were getting a financial handout from the work he put in.

Cooper is referring to the thirty-nine shareholders from the Johnston family who
employed Peter as their manager; although by the end of his forty-year tenure,
he and Nan had also been given shares, as part of the inducement to stay that
saw him remain on at Castlepoint for so long.

Gordon Meikle

Gordon Meikle first came to Castlepoint in 1951, as a contract fencer, and he was still working there when Emily and Anders Crofoot took over the property. There's a letterbox across the road from the station house with G Meikle on it, and his widow still lives in the house. Emily says that the knowledge and experience of working on Castlepoint Station that Gordon, along with Peter Laing, was able to provide were invaluable, and a huge part of making their transition work. A quiet and unassuming man, he often used to joke that the reason he'd stayed so long at Castlepoint was that he'd had a couple of good days when he first arrived and he's been waiting round for another one.

Through his early years at Castlepoint, Gordon was heavily involved in the land-clearing work undertaken in the 'fifties and was one of those interviewed for a *Country Calendar* programme, filmed soon after the Crofoots had bought Castlepoint. The issue of foreign ownership was seen as controversial and was addressed in the programme. At the time, there was wild talk about Lear jets landing on the airstrip and worried speculation about what it all might mean. When he heard that the station was up for sale and could be bought by Americans, Meikle agreed that at the time there was some concern.

'We didn't really know what was going to happen and certainly we studied the news with a certain amount of trepidation, because there was always that unknown factor, but after having met Emily and Anders and heard their ideas about the property, all that just disappeared and I can say without fear of contradiction that you couldn't have found better people.'

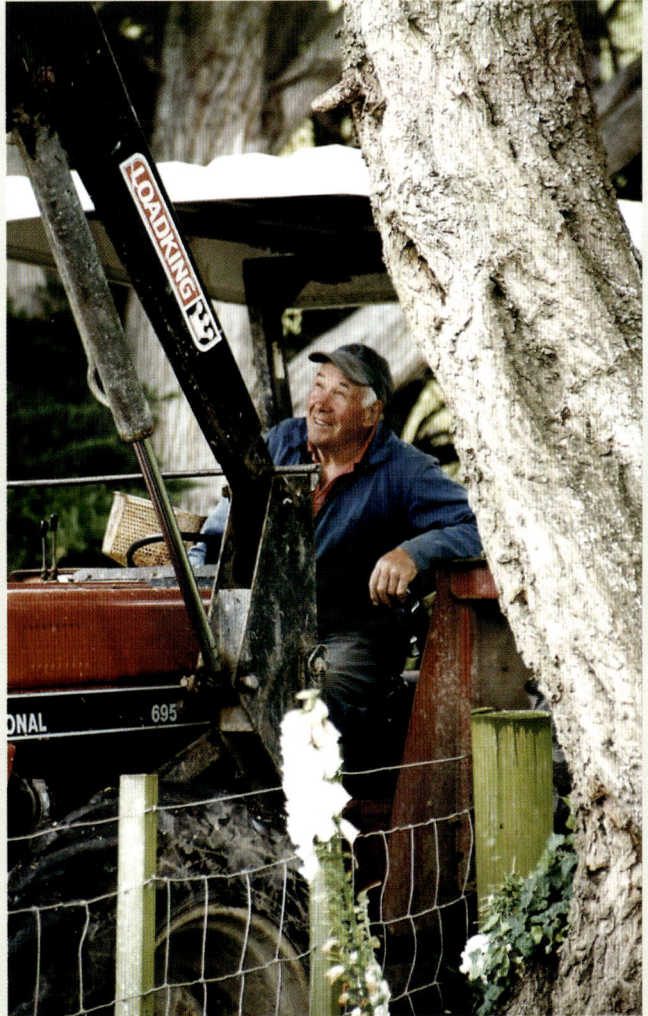

Opposite page: Looking out past the back-country at Wai Ngaio.

Above: Gordon Meikle, tractor driver and employee of Castlepoint Station for 60 years.

After Peter Laing retired in 1991, the station was run by manager Trevor Smyth, who provided the bridge between the Laing years and the modern era. Times were changing, and the demands on stations the size of Castlepoint, set up when labour was cheap and plentiful, led to a period of downsizing. By the time the station was eventually put on the market, it was ready for the next stage of its development, one that required a significant injection of capital.

While Peter Laing didn't always agree with the changes that came about as a result and readily spoke his mind, he was incredibly supportive of the new owners and was the one who introduced Anders Crofoot to the New Zealand Grasslands Association, of which he is now president. Both Emily and Anders feel a huge sense of gratitude for the firm foundation Peter left behind at Castlepoint.

According to Emily, 'We have gone on to the next stage of development, which Peter and Gordon both felt had to be done. Labour was cheap in their era, so the fact that we eliminated at least half the staff positions since Peter's time, through putting in the laneway [see page 132] and other labour-saving means, was a big deal. He would have had eight shepherds to do what we can now do with three.'

Peter Laing received an award in 2000 from the Castlepoint Progressive Association for his outstanding voluntary service to the people and district of Castlepoint, and in 2003 he received the Masterton District Council Civic Award for his service to the community at Castlepoint. His wisdom and counsel provided invaluable insights for the Crofoots; and his death, in 2004, at the age of seventy-four, saw the establishment of the Peter Laing Memorial Trust which provides financial assistance to aspiring young farmers from the Wairarapa. Peter's wife, Nan, passed away in 2008.

With Peter Laing's son Bill working with contracting and bulldozing and Fiona's daughter Cate a very good rider, Emily Crofoot sees Peter and Nan's skills carrying on with the next generation. There's a great deal of satisfaction in that, especially knowing that the Laing legacy is carrying on into the future on both the fronts which meant so much to Peter. 'I think that's really important — that both Castlepoint Station and the Laing family are continuing to go forward.'

Opposite page:
The strong and
the improvised —
gate fastenings at
Castlepoint Station.

Volunteer Firefighters

Following a long-standing local tradition, Anders Crofoot is fire chief of the local volunteer brigade, and there's a Commer truck doubling as a fire engine housed not too far away.

The Castlepoint Station staff and a few other local volunteers are specifically trained to deal with scrub and grass fires, which in a summer-dry area that rubs up against a large holiday-season population means they have to be on their toes. The large summer population doesn't always grasp the fact that there aren't convenient water sources at hand, which can sometimes present a challenge.

While eight crew members are trained, if an event occurs it is most often caused by holiday makers, and so willing hands are around and appear out of the woodwork to help. It goes with the territory out here, where the station has always provided a fire service for both the region and the settlement, originally using the big water tanker normally used for spraying gorse. The station also provides manpower for Search and Rescue as well as Civil Defence operations, as required.

John Broad was a volunteer in the 'fifties and 'sixties, and remembers that the first thing to be sent to a fire was the 200-gallon hormone sprayer full of water; then that would be backed up, if required, by the 5000-gallon tanker. In those days there was no fire station or official call-out system, and it was all hands to the pump. On race day, when the famous Castlepoint beach races were held (see page 173), the volunteers would have the hormone sprayer loaded with water, hooked up behind the tractor and parked by the woolshed all ready to go. Fortunately, the only fires John had to fight were at the rubbish tip, a grass fire behind the store and a few other smaller ones.

The 5000-gallon tank used to hold the underground diesel supply for the lighthouse keeper; when electricity came on it became surplus to requirements, and was purchased from the Marine Department by the station, along with a trailer.

Opposite page:
Anders Crofoot,
present-day fire
chief at Castlepoint.
Behind him is the
long-serving Commer
fire engine.

Braewold

While Thomas Guthrie was creating Castlepoint Station, Emily Crofoot's ancestors had already been farming for generations in New York State in the United States. Two very different families, on opposite sides of the world, were both engaged in the same pursuit — with no way of knowing that, in the future, their stories would come together in a most unexpected way.

THERE'S A QUOTATION AT THE START OF THIS BOOK which explains a great deal. From the minutes of the Bedford Farmers Club (New York State), the date is just one of the things that links it to the next chapter in Castlepoint's history.

That a group of farmers was discussing manure on New Year's Eve back in 1869 isn't the only astonishing thing. The other is that two farmers, James Wood and Thomas Guthrie — one living in the United States and the other in New Zealand — were contemporaries whose future stories would one day overlap.

Each man was deeply committed to the land. One was the steward of a long-standing farming heritage that stretched back to the very beginnings of farming settlement in the United States, which was then considered the 'New World'. The other was at the beginning of agriculture on a grand scale in the newest country of all — New Zealand — described famously by English writer Rudyard Kipling as 'Last, loneliest, loveliest, exquisite, apart …', which, when the first Maori colonizers arrived, became the most recent previously uninhabited large land mass to be occupied by humans.

Both men were farmers, and both had strong family values and an inherent understanding of the land. What would never have occurred to either of them, back in 1869, was that the story of both their families would eventually come together at Castlepoint.

Emily Crofoot's family first settled in America seven generations ago, where her forebears established a number of farms. The most recent, and the one that is most relevant to the story of Castlepoint Station, was Braewold, a 300-acre farm nestled into the countryside of Mount Kisco, in Westchester County, New York State.

Emily's family had been in the United States since 1638, when Jonas Wood emigrated from Halifax in England to settle in the Connecticut Valley. In time the English settlement moved to Long Island, and Jonas Wood became a commissioner, engaging in negotiations between the English and the Dutch settlers. In 1655 he purchased land on Long Island from the Native Americans, establishing a family home where he lived until his death by drowning, in 1660, in the Peconic River. His grandson came over to the mainland and settled northeast of Sing Sing, long before that name became synonymous with the now infamous prison.

Like many American families, the Woods' fortunes were disrupted by the Revolutionary War of Independence, when settlers were forced to choose where to place their allegiance — as Loyalists, with the English, or with the Revolutionaries. In the case of the Woods, they picked the losing side. As a result their lands were confiscated, and a branch of the family moved to Nova Scotia, where many other Loyalist families relocated.

Without their land, the Wood family was scattered in every direction. The first James Wood went to work for a blacksmith, Joseph Thorne, eventually marrying

his daughter Martha. By all accounts she was a strong and redoubtable woman with 'exceptionally good judgement, marked intellectual ability and an attractive personality'. While the Woods were raised as Presbyterians, the Thornes were Quakers, or members of the Society of Friends, and Martha was an Elder of the Chappaqua Monthly Meeting. After his marriage to Martha, James Wood also joined the Friends, beginning a long tradition of service to the community that continues today.

Strong, feisty women figure large in the history of Emily's family, not the least of whom was one named Sarah Field, a 'noble woman of fine character'. During

Braewold farm, New York State. *Crofoot family collection*

the Revolutionary War, a party of British soldiers drove off forty of her cattle to feed the army stationed in New York City. A few days later, she saddled her horse and rode forty miles to New York to demand payment, despite the strenuous efforts of her husband to dissuade her.

When stopped by an armed guard, who told her that she wasn't able to proceed without a pass, and he would have to shoot her if she did, she replied, 'Thee will do no such thing' and rode on. That she made it to the presence of the commanding general, Lord Howe, should come as no surprise. Here she immediately made her case.

'General Howe, thy men drove away forty head of our cattle. As thee is a gentleman, and, I trust, a Christian gentleman, I know thee will feel easier if thee pays for them, and I am here to furnish thee an opportunity for doing so.'

Clearly, she impressed Lord Howe, as well as piquing his curiosity, and after a long conversation she came away with the full value of her cattle in English gold. That the women in Emily Crofoot's family know the value of a good cattlebeast obviously goes without saying, and the skill has clearly made it down through the generations.

In 1809 the Wood family purchased Braewold, which the family continued to work until Emily's father, Jim Wood, decided that it was no longer viable as a family farm. By that stage seven generations of Jim's family had lived and worked at Braewold, but it was becoming increasingly difficult to maintain the farm, with rising real-estate values and six-storey apartment blocks a short distance away as the area became increasingly urbanized. New York City was spreading out; while Braewold had begun life as a farm in the country, now it was just an hour's drive from Central Park.

The only offspring of two generations, Jim balanced the family farm with a career as a financier and banker — and is fond of describing it as a situation where banking kept him solvent while farming kept him sane. But by the 1990s, farming in Mount Kisco was becoming increasingly difficult, with rapidly rising property values and land taxes. In the States, property taxes fund public education and can be prohibitive. At this stage, Emily and Anders were raising two young children at Braewold, David and Sarah. Emily had run the farm for six years while Anders worked as a financial analyst, often riding his bike to work, thirteen miles away. Apart from the growing difficulty of running the farm in an urban environment, the couple were concerned about the increasing materialistic influences surrounding their children as well as the erosion of the rural life they loved.

Opposite page: Emily's father, Jim Wood, reunited with his Ford Model A at Castlepoint.

Making Corn Pudding

One of the old American recipes that's on the menu at Castlepoint Station these days is corn pudding, and the method used to make it harks back to a long-gone age of homespun Yankee ingenuity and a Wood family tradition that's made it across to New Zealand.

Emily Crofoot still uses a corn scraper made by her grandfather, Hollingsworth Wood, from a diagram contained in an old cookbook she also still uses, the *Bedford Garden Club Cookbook*. Fresh ears of sweetcorn are first shucked, then the cobs are scraped vigorously against a series of nails and a back plate set into a wooden block, with the creamed corn falling out underneath — to be baked and served with some good station roast beef. It's delicious, and tastes nothing like the tinned variety it preceded.

While Sarah Crofoot describes it as a fair bit of effort to undertake to cook sweetcorn, it is one of the time-honoured traditions her family holds dear; and, as they say, the proof of the pudding is how it tastes — and this one tastes wonderful.

Braewold Corn Pudding

20-24 ears sweet corn

butter size of
walnut (about 2 tbsp.)

salt + pepper

Butter pyrex dish and <u>grate</u>
corn into it. Salt to taste, about
1 tsp.   butter
size of a walnut (about 2 tbsp.)
(If corn is old and dry, add about
1/2 cup milk - <u>no</u> egg.) Bake
at 375° - 400° for about 1 hour.
(grated corn may be frozen)

Mrs L. Hollingsworth Wood

Grate corn from
top to bottom of grater
pulling corn only
one direction

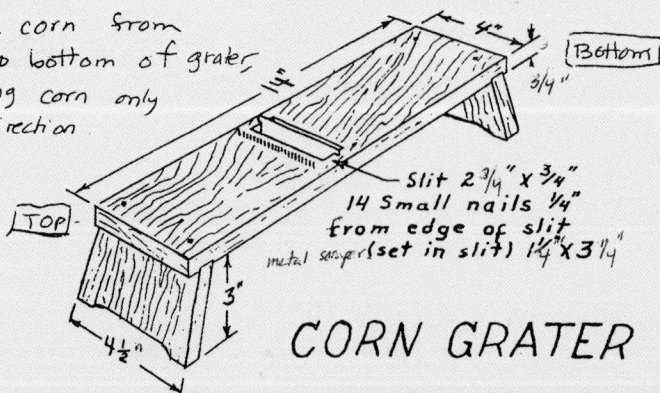

[Bottom]

3/4"

[TOP]

Slit 2¾" x ¾"
14 small nails ¼"
from edge of slit
metal scraper (set in slit) 1¼" x 3¼"

3"

4½"

CORN GRATER

Braewold was surrounded by multi-million-dollar homes and apartment blocks, and while their very long driveway kept the neighbours at a distance, and Emily cherished her agricultural roots and celebrated the rural traditions, the neighbourhood around the edges of the property was transforming.

'The area where both Emily and I grew up was changing tremendously and had become incredibly materialistic,' says Anders Crofoot. 'We didn't particularly like the values of most of the people there and we could see the kids were beginning to pick them up, so basically the decision was made to move them where we actually agree with the values.'

When Jim Wood made the decision to sell Braewold, it released capital for his two children, Emily and her brother Steve, to realize their own dreams of farming — and each went in a completely different direction. Steve moved to a property in Montana, and Emily and Anders were able to fulfil a childhood dream of Emily's: to farm in New Zealand.

And why New Zealand? Well, there's an amazing story behind that decision, one that many New Zealanders would relate to, involving OE, friendship and Scottish forebears.

Emily and Anders Crofoot at home in New Zealand, some 14,000 kilometres from their native New York.
Crofoot family collection

An Angus stud bull on the hill country at Castlepoint.

Friends and relations

As the Maori proverb tells us, the most important thing is people — he tangata, he tangata, he tangata. The friendship and web of connections made by two visiting cousins at a family reunion in Scotland would serve as the catalyst for a modern retelling of Thomas Guthrie's story. And the people who formed that web of association would prove to be invaluable, as the next chapter began to unfold for Castlepoint Station.

Previous page:
The Crofoots'
farm manager,
Stu Neal, with his
team of dogs at
Castlepoint.

Emily Wood in
November 1984,
by the wishing well
cave at Orakei
Korako Geyser,
near Taupo.
*Crofoot family
collection*

DONALD AND JILL COOPER AND EMILY AND ANDERS CROFOOT are long-standing friends — they share a wedding anniversary, Valentine's Day — and the couples have known each other since the 1980s; the women since the early 1970s. Their families are distantly related through the Douglas clan, and it was when Emily's grandfather was in Scotland and met a similarly travelling New Zealand Douglas, while both visited their ancestral home of Monymusk Castle, that the connection began. That was back in the 1940s, and the friendship has thrived and extended into a fourth generation.

At the time, overseas funds for Kiwis wanting to travel were difficult to get out of the country, and the American cousin, Hollingsworth Wood, invited the Kiwi cousin, Angus Douglas, to come to the United States as his sponsored guest. This was reciprocated, and an intergenerational web of friendship and cultural exchange saw a young Emily Wood become a frequent visitor to New Zealand while she was still in her teens and early twenties.

'My grandfather was visiting Monymusk at the same time as Jill's great-uncle, so my grandparents were friends with that generation, and my parents are friends with the next generation, Jill and I are friends as well — and our children are friends with their children. It's really nice that it's a four-generation connection.'

Emily came to New Zealand for the first time in 1973 with her parents and brother. She then visited in 1975 when she stayed for six months, working on farms in exchange for bed and board. In total she made three six-month visits, and applied to Lincoln College to study wool classing. She still has her rejection letter stating that they weren't able to educate overseas students. 'I figured that it was because I was the wrong sex and didn't drink enough, but it has been interesting to note how many of that Lincoln class have since become very good friends.'

Emily fell for New Zealand and the Kiwi way of farming in a big way. 'I definitely loved New Zealand; especially the fact that in the 'seventies, it was so different from what we were doing in agriculture on the east coast of America, which was basically preserving history. By the time we left Braewold, we had become an anachronism, making and carting hay through suburban traffic, whereas what we saw in New Zealand was that here agriculture was absolutely on the cutting edge of the world, doing embryo transfers. I certainly observed that agriculture had a voice in government and a very different power base, with so many of the politicians having a connection with the land, something we felt had been gone for several generations in the US. I found that very exciting and I knew it was where one day I wanted to be living and working.'

So, in a way, you could say the Crofoots didn't really emigrate — they just moved from one home to another.

Through the Kiwi connection, Emily had become good friends with Jill Douglas and the pair travelled together in the States and Canada. So when Jill married a farmer, it was no surprise to anyone who knew them that her husband, Donald Cooper, was one of the Kiwi farming mates who had helped Emily and Anders Crofoot find their way to Castlepoint; an important part of the New Zealand connection of friends, family and advisors who helped them make the move.

According to Emily, 'Jill and Donald Cooper are a big part of why we're at Castlepoint.' While Donald, now a member of the Castlepoint Advisory Board, doesn't see things being quite so clear cut, he does agree that, at the time, they had been keeping an eye out for Emily and Anders. 'This farm came on the market, and any time there was something we thought they might be interested in we'd let them know.'

The Crofoots were looking for a sheep and beef property, with a mixture of hills and flats, and while they had targeted the east coast region from South Canterbury to Hawke's Bay, they ideally wanted a coastal property. And New Zealand has a lot of coast.

What was about to unfold was a whirlwind — after two years of research and looking into a whole range of properties, Emily and Anders found out about Castlepoint Station.

The Coopers were full-time farmers themselves, at that stage farming near Taupo, although they are now on a good-rainfall property in Hawke's Bay. Donald came down and looked around Castlepoint with the Crofoots, who came to New Zealand after seeing a printed flyer and a promotional video, which had been shot coming off the back end of a drought. The sweeping helicopter shots of parched hill terraces led Emily's father Jim, a financier as well as a farmer, to wonder what on earth his daughter saw in the place — and how exactly she was planning to make a living from sand dunes. He needn't have worried. After looking at a century's worth of rainfall data, his daughter saw the same grey, over-grazed pastures and was determined never to let them get to that state ever again.

As Cooper describes it, 'Emily and Anders came over and said yes, this is the farm we want. It was eventually sold by private treaty, and once they'd bought it I then managed the transition until they were able to move to New Zealand a few months later. Because they purchased the company and there was a manager, Trevor Smyth, who kindly stayed on, they didn't need to move in right away.'

The Crofoots jointly applied for permanent residency, and, as Americans buying land in New Zealand, they needed permission from the Overseas Investment Commission, which came through in August. On 9 October the

Crofoots arrived, in time for docking, and, later, their first Kiwi Christmas.

Cooper had to guess what his friends would want to buy by way of stock and equipment. 'Then we had to do a physical count of the livestock, and I bought them a vehicle so that when they came to New Zealand they had something to get around in — a Mazda ute if I remember it rightly.'

Donald Cooper was one of the many people whose practical, solid, on-the-ground support made the Crofoots' transition from farming in New York State to farming on the East Coast of New Zealand happen. And this is ultimately a story about a family, because through the family connection Jim Wood asked him to 'keep an eye on the farm and keep an eye on the kids'. As a result, when they set up a board of advisors, Donald Cooper was one of those making up the board and is also a family trustee for young David Crofoot.

Asked about the main challenges at the time for the new owners, Cooper is direct. 'The main challenge they were always going to face is that east-coast New Zealand is going to be dry in the summer — you can have a lot of grass here and two weeks later it can fry and blow away. This is good stock country, and grows healthy stock, though it has its difficulties. The farm had been run as a big station, with managers since the mid-1800s, so there was potential for further development, but it was expensive development, and that had to be managed and planned.'

As Cooper puts it, 'The challenges never stop with agriculture — you can't manage the weather, unfortunately — so we manage what we can control and we try to plan for the rest, and then have a plan in place that is also hopefully an escape route; although we don't always get it right.'

There was an extra challenge lying in wait for the Americans, and it was one Cooper admits he never envisaged would become one of the biggest personal problems Emily would have to deal with — responsibility for the weight of history an iconic property like Castlepoint Station carried.

'When they first arrived they were constantly faced with people coming and saying, "Look, I've done this for years" and when they checked they'd find people were just trying it on half the time, that is if they showed you the courtesy of calling in.'

And some of the requests take your breath away. It was not just access to the station but demands to keep holiday-makers' horses and dogs, or coming home to find strangers playing tennis on your tennis court, or people wanting to put their fishing berley in the station freezer or land their private plane on your airstrip. One person actually stopped Emily, who was riding her horse on the beach, and asked her to get off so his kids could have a ride.

Two-tooth ewes (12–18 months old) and their lambs prior to weaning on Loafer's Flat.

As Anders Crofoot describes it, 'By the end of that first summer it was just horrendous and we rang up our lawyer and asked if we had bought a public park or if we actually had any property rights? What was most disheartening was that many people were just trying us on. At one point we were joking about putting in an answering phone with press 1 for Emily, press 2 for Anders, press 3 for David, press 4 for Sarah and press 5 if you "always have". Because without fail when somebody rang up and wanted to do something and you'd say no, they'd say, "But I always have", then when you track it down it would turn out that on one occasion three years ago they'd been along as a friend of a friend.'

Eventually, Emily and Anders had to stick a peg in the ground and close the station to casual visitors. 'After that first summer we sat down and put an access policy in place,' Anders explains. 'We stopped individual recreational access. However, several times a year we give access to community and agricultural groups, for example a four-wheel-drive convoy going through raising money for a local school, horse treks for the hunt club, and recently, six busloads of Farm Foresters on a national conference, so that we give some public access in a controlled fashion, and Castlepoint can be shared as a community treasure. Occasionally, we get requests from people on a journey — we had a father and son riding up the East Coast together, or a guy who was running down the coast from Cape Reinga — if somebody is doing a journey of epic proportions like that and they give us advance warning, then generally we say yes. What we don't find workable is people just wanting to go out for recreational reasons and have a picnic on what is a working farm.'

At the time, Emily was quoted as saying, 'We want to be an active part of the community, but we didn't put an enormous amount of money on the line and change our lives and where we live to buy a public park — we're trying to run a 27,000-stock-unit business.' What she also said, and which cuts to the core of the issue — and it was a big issue at the time — was: 'We feel it is a privilege to be on Castlepoint Station, and we want our visitors to also understand that it is a privilege, and not *as of right*.'

It was a difficult period for them, and for a while for the community too, as adjustments were made. 'I felt very sorry for Emily at the time,' says Donald Cooper. 'Castlepoint was a beach community *and* a working farm *and* a holiday park — and there had been a culture of access, with managers often more inclined to say yes when they really should have said no, in order to avoid ripples in the community. But it's been very well managed since then, and it's now all in the past.'

At the end of the day, in this country we're all immigrants or the children of immigrants, and there's still an underlying respect for people who do a hard day's work. The Crofoots didn't take long to show they were those kind of folks, and that they meant what they said about making the business work, from the ground up.

One of the things they said when they came here, and first met Trevor Smyth, the manager, who was understandably a bit nervous about what having new American owners living on site would mean, was: 'We're happy to pick up some staples and a hammer and go and fix fences if we need to; we're not going to be here telling you what to do all the time.'

Since then Emily and Anders have gained an immense knowledge of New Zealand agriculture. Emily participates in many farming groups and Anders reads widely and is involved in the more technical side of things, such as the New Zealand Grasslands Association, and as a result they now have as great a knowledge, if not a greater one, than many other New Zealand farmers.

Cooper sees this thirst for knowledge and the determination to run Castlepoint Station as a successful business as paramount: 'Because this farm could gobble you up. Talking about iconic stations, most of these iconic stations you come across have been iconic because they've been big, but now with the changing cost structure you've *got* to farm as a business or they become a big hole. Most of the big farms now are run by families with other financial interests.'

Cooper now sees that having experienced individuals like himself, Ashburton-based farm advisor John Tavendale and, in the early days, Johnny Ackland, the owner of Mount Peel Station, who is both a friend and a large-scale business owner, on the ground and on Emily's side was absolutely fundamental: 'Although Emily knew a lot about agriculture when she arrived, over here it's totally different. But they've both worked hard to get where they are, they've become part of farm discussion groups — they have groups here, they go over to other people's farms and that's how you learn. Everybody does things a particular way for different reasons. The good thing that happens here is that they talk through things. At the end of the day we only act as an advisory board, it's Emily and Anders who make the decisions — it's their business — they can do what they like.'

It is clear from talking to Donald Cooper that while Peter Laing's time at Castlepoint left long shadows, there have also been a lot of changes since those days. One of the main differences between the Laing days and now lies in the stock itself. 'Here at Castlepoint they've changed the breed a bit as performance parameters have changed. Peter ran both Romneys and a development flock of Perendale ewes.'

The Laneway

One of the changes Peter Laing certainly scratched his head over was the introduction of the laneway, something everyone at the station now uses daily, and it comes up again and again whenever anyone is talking about the changes the Crofoots have instigated. The concept certainly isn't new — it's been around for a long time — but it was new to Castlepoint and revolutionized stock movement around the property; in fact, every aspect of moving around the property, people included.

In simple terms, a broad gravel road was built from one end of the property to the other, and past the new woolshed which is located internally on the property. This building serves as the local tsunami evacuation centre, as it's on very high ground with potentially spectacular and extremely safe views of any incoming tidal waves. In all, a total of more than 17 kilometres of fenced and gated private road was constructed through the heart of the long, narrow station, cutting across hilltops, through valleys and in part along the coastal strip. It's wide enough to comfortably drive a mob of cattle or a herd of sheep along, and there's a speed limit of 30 kilometres per hour, with convenient paddocks along the way to put the stock in if you need to hold them overnight.

The laneway replaced a tortuous track along the coast which ran through large paddocks and therefore was difficult for moving large mobs. This did away with the multiple-day muster that was often the only way to move stock across country — with men, dogs and horses.

'Before we arrived, the access was down the old coastal track made of slippery clay. If you came through the middle of the station, along tracks, you were going through stock and disturbing them many times a day. While the clay tracks were fine on quads, in the winter, when they were wet, you couldn't take anything bigger than a quad on them,' remembers Anders Crofoot. 'With no stock laneway on a long, narrow property your ability to move stock was actually quite restricted, especially when you no longer had a large group of shepherds at your disposal.'

They built the laneway using material from five separate quarries on station land, where deposits of rotten rock were found which proved to be suitable for crushing into road metal. A massively expensive undertaking, both in time and labour and in dollars, the laneway has quickly become integral to the running of the modern station, and began to pay its way with the very first sheep truck that was able to drive through the station to collect lambs, ready for sale and in prime condition.

'When you're shipping lambs out and you're paid on a live-weight basis, they could lose up to a kilogram each just from dehydration, by the time you've driven them to where the stock trucks used to have to meet the mobs — whereas now we can wean the lambs first thing in the morning, then in the afternoon the trucks come and pick them up right away so there's a payback quite quickly.'

Revolutionizing stock movement, the laneway at Castlepoint. In the background is the Ngakawau whare, once the staging post for shepherds, dogs and horses working the remote areas of the station, now disused.

The huge expense has been judged worth it, even though it took time to construct — over two years, and through some extremely difficult country. As Anders explains, 'Now it's possible to take a stock truck and trailer right to the stock — not the other way round.'

While realizing that, in general, farming has had to become more scientific in an evolving world where markets and consumer demands are constantly changing, the Castlepoint team have had to accept that the East Coast of New Zealand — with a finely balanced ecology and vulnerable soils — is not the best place to be experimenting too much too soon.

As Cooper puts it: 'After all, you can have all the best technology and advice in the world and the weather will still break you or make you. While Castlepoint Station might not be leading innovators, I'd like to think we can be fast followers.

'One of the biggest changes here in the last few years is that we've finally got the stock looking really good all the time — the farm manager, Stu Neal, and his team do a fantastic job. They've had very good managers here and everyone has added their bit to the operation, but it's taken a while and now it's very seldom that I come down and think — ooh, that stock's struggling.'

The key to this, in Cooper's mind, is having a plan and managing the farm, in the sense that if the season goes against you, you have a plan in place to cope with that, each year adding more data and more information to the pool of knowledge that defines this particular farm, this particular set of soil, terrain, wind and weather patterns. Emily Crofoot came to Castlepoint from managing a farm that had been in her family for seven generations, and the accumulation of knowledge in that time was immense; at Castlepoint, they had to start that process all over again, and by learning the hard way.

'In farming you learn by your mistakes, and — as I'm fond of telling people — in this business, if you're getting it right seventy per cent of the time you're doing well; seventy-five to eighty per cent and you've cracked it, but don't beat yourself up if you don't make one hundred per cent because you never will, and if you do, then you're not being honest about something!'

In many examples in the recent past, large rural properties have experienced difficulties when the generations change, with younger folk often not wanting to have the lives their parents experienced on the land, turning their back on several generations of family ownership and leaving the land. In some cases, the properties involved are isolated, which has been part of the problem. 'But in recent years I think that's been starting to change — and suddenly there's a lot of younger ones going back onto the big farms, with families retaining control.'

In Cooper's opinion, that's when farms like Castlepoint are at their most successful. 'We've seen the corporate model introduced in a lot of places, and it's worked dismally in some and struggled in others. It works well with the dairy model, but in the sheep and beef model, there's nothing that beats the hands-on approach. Take this place — Emily and Anders don't know everything but they're setting structures in place that work, surrounding themselves with good managers and good staff and making it attractive for them to be here.'

Opposite page: Angus cows with Charolais crossbred calves.

Left: Born of the hill country, a spring lamb at Castlepoint.

Making the move

'While we didn't realize it at the time, we had brought the children from the cold and darkness of a North American winter into the warmth and sunlight of a New Zealand summer. The contrast was amazing, and somehow magical. I will never forget the look on Sarah's face when she was able to walk out and pick a ripe grapefruit from the tree for her breakfast, in what should have been the middle of winter.'

Emily Crofoot

THE CROFOOTS BROUGHT SOME HIGHLY DESIRABLE SKILLS with them when they
moved to New Zealand in 1998 — Emily had a strong farming background,
and Anders had a double degree (in computer science and psychology) from
Dartmouth College, New Hampshire, part of the Ivy League. Anders also has
many practical multi-tasking abilities, some gained as a college student. 'When
I was at university I started off washing dishes and waiting tables at a restaurant
where I worked my way up through the ranks, so that by the time I graduated
I'd spent eighteen months basically running the "back of the house", doing all the
ordering, organizing cooking shifts and floor managing.

'Before Emily and I got married we'd discussed the possibility of emigrating.
Emily had come out to New Zealand when she was younger and fallen in love
with the country and had always been trying to figure out a way to create a life
here. At Braewold I'd met a lot of the Kiwis who were either friends or family,
or both, when they were visiting, and I first came out to New Zealand in 1987
on our honeymoon.'

While he was working at the restaurant, Anders had computerized their
operation, something he was to repeat at other workplaces and which eventually
led to him going out on his own as a computer consultant. So when he came to
Castlepoint and found a very rudimentary use of computers, it wasn't long before
he began to make his mark, and now the station's sophisticated set-up and strong
commitment to technology is one of its attractions for staff.

'In 1998 the station was using the accounting program Cashmanager, which in
simple terms meant the station manager entered basic accounts information into
the system, and this was then taken to an accountant in Masterton for processing.
We've always believed that doing your own business accounts is one of the best
ways of learning what's going on. When we were looking at buying the station, one
of the first things we noticed was what they were paying the accountant, and we
figured that if things went badly we could live on that — so as soon as we arrived
I took over doing the accounts and the payroll and I've carried on.'

By the time the Crofoots arrived, the station badly needed an injection of
capital, something that Anders could see would have been difficult under the
previous ownership structure. 'At the time they had multiple shareholders, and,
although the station had been paying dividends, at that point in the late 'nineties
you had a sharemarket that had been going ballistic for years and people were
beginning to expect fifteen to twenty per cent returns on their invested capital.
With Castlepoint they would have been looking at an asset worth millions of
dollars on the books, but only returning what a typical sheep and beef station
returns, which is one to three per cent, and because none of the owners was living

here, the connection with the land had become pretty remote. It seemed to be the right time for them to take their money and do something else with it. From our point of view it was great, since otherwise we wouldn't have had this opportunity.'

As Emily describes it, 'When Anders and I were wrestling with how we were going to tackle this project, we often mused that much of his world was in the twenty-first century and much of my world was in the nineteenth century, so I would say that what he brought were the twenty-first-century skills in terms of quantitative analysis, mapping and electronic communications systems and all of that, while I brought nineteenth-century skills in terms of love of hard work and understanding stockmanship, horses, growing crops and the logistics of how things needed to come together.'

Sarah's brother, David, an accomplished surfer at his favourite stomping ground, The Gap at Castlepoint.
Silas Hansen

This led to the couple's decision to divide their areas of responsibility into 'animate' and 'inanimate', with Emily looking after the animate — human resources and livestock; and Anders the inanimate — technology, development and finance. 'He also has things like gorse, which technically is living, but as we want it dead, it goes on his list.'

As it turned out, 1998 was a very favourable time to have bought a farming property, as the Crofoots were selling their assets in a high-performing economy and buying into New Zealand's East Coast, which was coming off the back of several seasons of drought. And, as they say, timing is everything — in this case it meant the difference between buying Castlepoint Station or a smaller operation, as in the two years they took to do their research, the Kiwi dollar kept dropping. 'When we started to look for a New Zealand property, the Kiwi dollar was at 70 cents US and when we actually purchased and traded the dollar was at 51 cents, so all of a sudden it meant a huge difference in what we had available to invest.'

Originally, Emily and Anders had intended to buy a property with around 10,000 stock units, which would give them some scale and the capacity to employ at least one other person, because at that stage they didn't know if Anders' telecommuting would leave him much time to work on the farm. As Emily puts it: 'As the company only wanted his head, they didn't particularly care where he sat!'

When the Crofoots moved to Castlepoint, and put their assets and their family's life on the line, despite having friends and extended family all over New Zealand they literally only knew six other people in the Wairarapa — and that included the real-estate agent.

Because the manager had agreed to stay on for the first twelve months, they were able to spend time adjusting to life in the Wairarapa and concentrate on things like remembering to stay on the left-hand side — not only on the road but also in the aisles of supermarkets and on the sidewalk, which they learned was called a footpath. 'We also learned that there's a whole other language, such as you buy things at a chemist, not a pharmacy!'

While Emily can recall moments when she knew other properties weren't right, the sale of Castlepoint came about so quickly that it's difficult to single out any one moment of recognition, a point when she knew this would be her new home.

'There was another large coastal property on the market at the same time and I'll never forget when the fax came through, stating that bovine tuberculosis had been detected in the property. I just said then that my line had been crossed, as it would be too hard to manage and I couldn't see the property ever eliminating TB. I've since been proven wrong, but at the time I said no; we have choices. There were similar moments with other properties, but with Castlepoint it was two and a half weeks from when we first saw the brochure to having an accepted offer, and that included a trip down here.

'In reality, from the moment we saw the brochure we said, "This may be it", and from then on that initial feeling was consistently reinforced. We'd been sent a sales video and we'd watched it so many times we'd memorized it, so by the time we came here everything was already feeling familiar. I remember we came to look at the property and our good friend Donald was with us, and Derek Daniel had been asked to come along because he was a good farmer and from the Wairarapa. One of the directors was also with us, as was the realtor and the farm manager. We were at the holiday park, up by Cabin Nine, looking out towards the lighthouse. They all said, "Isn't it beautiful?" '

But the banker's daughter was desperately trying to avoid looking at the vista, trying hard not to be swayed by what was in front of her. 'I said I need to keep my eyes on the ground and focus on the financial performance, but really I was just blown away, it was so beautiful and the scale was just mind-boggling!' Emily will admit that the infamous wind took a bit of getting used to but, she says, 'It literally felt right from the time we first saw the brochure — and it has always felt right since.'

Some places just do things to your heart — you see them and it's like something sings, a feeling Emily had about the land here, right from the beginning.

'We feel privileged to be the current stewards of Castlepoint Station and we see that as both an opportunity and an obligation. That is why it was very important to us that the history be written down both in terms of our commitment to Nan and Peter Laing, who were so wonderful to us, but also in terms of the importance of seeing that history and that era of New Zealand farming recorded for posterity. Much of what we do in terms of our involvement with the community is because we feel it's all part of being the stewards of Castlepoint Station, and everyone pulling together is what makes communities thrive.'

It's ironic to remember that at one point the Crofoots were viewed as 'the foreign owners', although in fact, after 123 years of ownership by the Johnston family, of the 39 shareholders in Castlepoint, many were living in the United Kingdom and had been for some time. The Crofoots, on the other hand, became New Zealand citizens in 2002, as soon as they could.

'When we arrived we were very grateful for comments two friends made — one was that Kiwis will always give you a chance, and it's up to you to blow it. I was very grateful for that observation; and second was from a business advisor who told us that in true tall-poppy fashion, "There are people waiting for you to trip up." To that we said, "OK that's the lay of the land, we'll keep our head down and get on with learning and working, and we'll be very careful not to make decisions for the sake of making our mark, knowing that new brooms also lose some good dust." And what we've learned, with an operation this size, is that it's safer to go a bit slower, because you can go too fast and when you go off the rails on this scale it's like trying to steer the *Titanic*. You just can't go as fast as one can in a smaller, more nimble, operation, but we're getting there.'

What the Crofoots found was a station in transition, stripped back from the era when Castlepoint Station had had a staff of about fifteen to a much smaller, leaner and meaner staff. It was essentially the same transition that was going on everywhere at the time, and Peter Laing's successor, manager Trevor Smyth, had taken the station through quite a modernization process. Anders recalls that when they arrived it was already a very pared-down operation, 'The station's performance had been winding back and basically they'd gotten to a certain point and then struck droughts and an infestation of porina, and a few other things. Trevor did some very good work here but the station was at the point where it was ready for another stage of development.'

Emily feels that the base of the station is very strong as a result of the early development work done: 'We credit a tremendous amount to the likes of Peter Laing and Gordon Meikle, who literally gave their lives to do the hard yards.'

Sun setting behind baches, pohutukawa and the station hill country beyond.

And make no mistake: that's what it takes, and what it has always taken to tame this country. This land along the East Coast — summer-dry land that literally soaks up everything you give it — is very demanding.

As Emily is quick to point out, 'You look at many of the Wairarapa coastal properties and certainly in my observation, Castlepoint is the clearest and probably the only property which has consistently kept on top of its development, maintaining it since the 1960s — which is no mean feat. All you have to do is look at properties that have reverted back to scrub to realize what an incredible job that was. As a result, the foundation is there, the soil fertility is there and when we came here we made a conscious decision to invest in infrastructure, and invest upfront much as a dairy farm does.'

The result of that surge of investment was the laneway, the subdivision fencing, changes to the water system, improving staff housing, and building additional stock-handling facilities.

Despite moderate forecast revenue projections for increasing the annual earning ability of the property, the first flush of enthusiasm was followed by a period of intense concern, as discouragement set in after three years of falling product prices. Following all of that they realized that, on paper anyway, they had put their family's financial assets, the result of generations of hard work, marginally at risk. 'We became very aware of why, traditionally, sheep and beef farmers funded development out of cash flow. I would say that the absolute low for me was when we had to borrow money to pay the interest on the development loans. Even though this was only short term, and timing-related, it was a horrible sinking feeling which required asking ourselves if we had taken our heritage, which had enabled us to do this massive undertaking of investment for the future, and actually put it in jeopardy. Fortunately, the answer was no, we hadn't.'

As Anders describes it, the family made the move and followed it up with a significant investment in development — and just when everything was supposed to start paying off, the industry went sideways and backwards for four years. The investment in the future of the property was about putting money into new fencing, new tracks, the laneway; things which were done to improve the earning ability. 'And the good thing is that these things don't disappear, and now that earlier work is starting to pay off. Coming from a farming background, and also coming off a family farm where our kids were the seventh generation, means that for us taking a long-term view comes as second nature.'

One of the things Anders remembers having to learn quickly was how to deal with winter mud. 'I'd grown up in the northeast of the United States where you have snow and ice, but I'd never really dealt with driving through mud, which is a whole lot more difficult. By comparison, snow and ice are actually quite predictable. While we were learning how to ride quads, we managed to roll them a few times that first year — fortunately, nobody got hurt.'

For the Crofoot children, Sarah, who was eight, and David, who was ten when they moved to New Zealand, the change was dramatic — going from a school with 300-plus pupils to a single-teacher school with a roll of seven, and from snow and ice in winter to summer sun and living by the sea. David, in particular, felt as though his parents had taken him to the end of the earth. At the time he was very interested in skateboarding, so Emily and Anders built some ramps for him so that he could carry on practising his skills, despite there being only sand and dust where he'd been used to roads and concrete at home in the States.

'It was very interesting that by 2000 when the Olympics were in Sydney, they were only interested in New Zealand athletes,' remembers Emily. 'In June of that year we went back to the States and he met up with his mates — and then he realized his skateboarding training in the backblocks of New Zealand had kept him at a skill level with his friends. Even better, his friends were all jealous of the fact that he had a motorbike and the sea was at his back door. That was a real turning point for him — whereas Sarah was young enough that she just immediately adapted.'

Now David has a wicked Kiwi accent, and says new friends are often surprised to learn he was born in the States and still carries an American passport. He hopes to put that to good use and plans to do some travelling in the United States once he's finished studying. A graduate of the Raglan Surfing School, he's clearly made the most of the opportunity living by the sea at Castlepoint gave him to take up a new sport, once he'd exhausted the limited possibilities of skateboarding.

Both Crofoot children are completing degrees, and both have some great friends. Sarah is a regional hockey rep, having played for Wairarapa and now Central Districts, right up to National Hockey League level. This followed many years competing with her horses; David is a dead-keen surfer, and is passionate about the surfing opportunities Castlepoint has to offer.

A strong sense of family has meant that while the children were growing up on the other side of the world from their grandparents, Twink and Jim Wood — Emily's high-octane octogenarian parents — have made it their practice to come down to New Zealand every summer, staying for two to three months. While Sarah has no doubt she'll end up back at Castlepoint, she's also keen to follow her grandfather into the world of high finance, with a particular interest in international trade and banking. David's keen to travel a bit before he decides what he wants to do, and the amount that they have already travelled is something both younger Crofoots are aware sets them aside from some of their mates.

As Sarah puts it, 'My friends are talking about doing their OE and I'm thinking, *I've already done a lot of travelling in my life* — my other grandparents moved to Portugal just before we came to New Zealand, and we have visited them there. Our good friends, the Rushtons, sailed around the world with their parents on a yacht for five years, and we visited them in Australia, Thailand, Greece and Tahiti, so I'm aware that compared to many of my friends I've already seen quite a bit of the world.'

Like other young people who've grown up on Castlepoint Station, Sarah and David have done their share of work around the place, and in Sarah's case, more formally as part of fulfilling her degree requirements from Massey University, where she is studying AgriBusiness.

Sarah credits her parents with making the 'real world' much easier for her: 'We always had a family saying: "Defend your position". What this meant was that any statement you made, you had to defend, because Mum would grill you on it — and she always said that when we went out to the real world after growing up here, it would be much easier, and she was right. We always had to think about things because we knew that if we made a statement about something we were going to be asked a million questions about it, so having to do that in the real world now comes as second nature.'

The children never found it difficult to make friends, something Sarah credits to the fact that small rural towns are close-knit anyway. As far as other children were concerned, they were just 'another couple of kids'.

'Lots of decision-making and thinking at Castlepoint takes place over the dinner table. It's good now that we're older and having grown up with all of the discussions, we take it for granted. At uni a lot of the things I'm studying now are what I've been learning about since I was ten. You've just been exposed to things without even knowing, like learning a new language by immersion; you didn't even notice you were learning but it's paying dividends. Previously, I didn't really like the focus on the farm and I used to challenge my parents to get through a whole dinner without talking about the farm, and they couldn't.'

David's surfing photos, along with Sarah's hockey and eventing ribbons, are testament to how successfully they have made the transition, and their enthusiastic approach to life is the embodiment of one of the thoughts that Anders expressed about coming to New Zealand: 'There used to be something called Yankee ingenuity. You don't hear very much about that any more, but you still do hear about Kiwi ingenuity … figuring your own way out of problems, not sitting round waiting for somebody else to solve them for you, and we thought being brought up surrounded by that thinking would be the best thing we could do for our kids.'

Emily treasures a memory of being invited to dinner by one of their neighbours, where she met another guest, a very established fifth-generation Kiwi. During the course of the evening she talked about the time she was working for a fencing contractor on a farm in the South Island, and doing a shearing course at Tolaga Bay and one thing and another. 'And he said to me, "You're not an American, you're a bloody Kiwi!" I thought that was very high praise.'

Opposite page: The end of a day's stock work at Castlepoint's Otahome yards.

Shorn ewe hoggets ready for vaccinating, prior to lambing.

Surfing at Castlepoint

In a region with high winds and a long coastline, it's not surprising to learn that surfing is one of the attractions that continues to draw people to Castlepoint — after all, they get some awesome waves here, and the area is featured in the *New Zealand Surfing Guide*, which lists a number of beaches in the area.

The Whakataki Hotel is a well-known surfing centre which has traditionally welcomed surfers and surf clubs over the years, and is renowned for having good spot breaks right in front. Surfers who come here are told to expect a left-hand reef break with an optimum wave size of 1 to 3 metres.

Castlepoint beach itself is a good place for surfers of all levels, although high tide can often be too full, causing the beach to close out. There's a variable break in front of the store and the camping ground, known to produce both left and right peaks.

The Gap, which in surfing terms can be described as a narrow inlet featuring a beach break set-up, is located in Deliverance Cove. With the shelter provided by the bulk of Castle Rock and the reef, it can often have the best surfing conditions, especially when strong winds are making everywhere else unsurfable. The best time to get into the water is when there's a solid swell running, when surfers can expect to find grunty left and right peaks, long workable walls and the odd tube section.

The sand here is amazingly fine — and you might find you have to share the water with seals. Good advice is to stick to the dark, wet sand on the walk out to the Gap, and the natural amphitheatre provided by the sand dunes makes it an incredibly beautiful place to take to the water.

About fifteen minutes' walk over the saddle from The Gap is Christmas Bay, which features a beach break. This area is usually a lot less crowded, described by surfing guidebooks as isolated and a south swell magnet. It's particularly good when the winds are north to northeast.

Opposite page, top: A busy day at The Gap, a sheltered inlet harbouring one of Castlepoint's best surfing spots.

Bottom: A typical bach by the beach at Castlepoint, with an unobstructed view of the tides and sunrise.

Angus breeding cows and their calves awaiting stock rotation.

Emily's reality: living with multiple sclerosis

'For years I'd been looking forward so much to being able to get back onto the land in a physical way; to have my own dog to work, and go riding on the beach and the hills. Suddenly, it wasn't going to happen and I had to accept that my reality would be very different from my dream.'

Emily Crofoot

✦

Previous page: Tall
fescue grass gone
to seed in summer.

COMING TO FARM IN NEW ZEALAND HAS BEEN EMILY'S LIFELONG DREAM, ever
since she first came to New Zealand as an eighteen-year-old, fresh from high
school. When she and Anders were finally able to turn that dream into a reality,
she had no idea that things would turn out to be very different to her expectations.

'I've always been a hard-working, physically active person and longed to be
part of a farming operation which made sound commercial sense. There was so
much to learn and do when we first moved to New Zealand that I tended to put
off doing things just for fun to the phase of life when I wouldn't be tied to school
schedules, and would finally have time to get out there and ride my horse all
over the property and do the work I love to do … I was greatly looking forward to
having the time to actually work consistently my heading dog. I think the fact that
this is now not going to happen is different from what I expected — not better or
worse, just different.'

Emily Crofoot at
her piano in the
homestead. Despite
being diagnosed
with multiple
sclerosis in 2002,
Emily continues
to persevere both
with running the
farm and with her
long-held musical
prowess.

What these words don't fully communicate is what happened a few years
after the Crofoots had committed to a life in New Zealand. 'When we arrived, the
children were quite young and our first priority was their assimilation into the

community and being involved with the school. We also had business obligations in Masterton and, because of the time that took, being an hour away, our days were often quite broken up. I had always envisioned that I would really get going with my involvement with the physical work on the farm once the children were older, but this was not meant to be as I was diagnosed with multiple sclerosis in 2002. I developed optic neuritis, which is often the first sign. This happens when there's a demyelinating incident of the optic nerve, and I temporarily lost vision in my left eye for a few weeks.'

Because the disease presents so differently in each person, nobody knew what form it would take. 'I was very fortunate to not only be working with a neurologist here in New Zealand, but also one in the United States. This way, I could make sure I was up to speed with whatever was happening in the world.'

It took Emily quite a while to come to terms with the fact that multiple sclerosis can be described as a random disease. It's considered most likely to be viral in origin, and although one needs to have a genetic predisposition to allow the virus to enter your body, it's pretty much the luck of the draw who gets it. 'It wasn't my behaviour, or choices I had made, so it wasn't so much *Why me?* as *This wasn't in the ten-year plan!* — so for quite a while I chose to get on with life and not make it my focus, which was actually recommended: don't worry about what might be, just get on with what you can do.'

There are two main types of multiple sclerosis: relapsing/remitting, which is the more common form where sufferers have an attack and then rebuild almost, but not quite, back to the point they were before the attack; and progressive, where it just steadily deteriorates.

'Unfortunately, I have the progressive form, and that's the kind that is least responsive to medication, so we've tried some different therapies and at this point we're just managing it. I feel very, very fortunate to be in a loving family and in a job where I can do as much or as little as I am able, with people around who will pick up the pieces and take over things I can't do, or back off and let me do things I can do when it's a good day.'

Her limitations are a reality Emily can't avoid, and instead she's found ways of accommodating the illness and its effects. The two biggest issues she faces are lack of balance and fatigue. 'With the lack of balance, I do fall a fair bit and I try wherever possible not to put myself into a situation where that can cause a problem; for example, I very rarely go in a pen with stock any more. I have a crutch, which I use mostly on uneven ground, but I don't use it in the house where the surfaces are more predictable; whereas if I'm going outside and I'm on uneven surfaces I take my crutch.'

There's a stair lift fitted in the stairway up to the office, and while Emily usually tries not to use it unless she has to, lately she's been quite tired and has tended to use it more.

'That's a wonderful story — a lady I barely know moved into a house with a stair lift in it that she didn't need, and she offered it to the occupational therapist at the hospital for anyone who might need it who wouldn't otherwise qualify for government assistance. I was very fortunate that my occupational therapist thought of me and I feel very privileged to have it.

'The other thing that's really wonderful is what I call my turbocharger — a Bioness unit. I was the first person in New Zealand to be able to buy one of these and it's a miracle of modern technology, which straps around my calf. There's a gait sensor that sits underneath my heel and as I lift my heel it uses Bluetooth technology to send a signal to two electrodes, one of which is on my nerve and the other one is on my muscle. It gives me a zap, like I'm attached to an electric fence, and it helps my foot lift and helps prevent my foot from dragging. I've got my little control unit here, on my belt, so when I'm outside and walking I'll always have that on.'

While Emily has always been very involved with spinning and weaving, and was even apprenticed to a German master weaver for a while, her multiple sclerosis has had an impact on that part of her life. 'Although I could dedicate the time [to her textile art], I now have trouble with my right side, both arm and leg. I only have X amount of energy and I have to make choices. I'm not convinced that weaving and spinning is probably a good use of my limited hand motions.'

That, and not being able to garden, are the only hints of regret she allows herself. While you'll never catch Emily Crofoot feeling sorry for herself, she will admit to finding 'being dependent' personally very frustrating. 'Knowing that something needs to be done and having to ask somebody to do it. Although everybody in my world is willing to help, it comes at the cost of them not being able to do something they want to do.'

There's no doubt that having multiple sclerosis has changed Emily Crofoot's life considerably, and her determination to carry on without compromising the lives of those around her is admirable, if not always easy for her family and friends. 'But you'll never change that,' says her daughter Sarah, 'and if you tried, she'd use up even more energy fighting against it.'

Perhaps there is no surprise that the strong, feisty, independent nature of the women in Emily Crofoot's family is coming to the fore again.

Opposite page:
A bed of smooth beach rocks along the foreshore at Castlepoint.

Happy campers

For many in Wellington, and in the Wairarapa in particular, Castlepoint means first and foremost a summer beach and a holiday camp, where long golden summers are spent filled with sun, sand and seaspray. How the holiday park came to be is a fascinating story from the era when Kiwis got stuck in, and made things happen — and shows that even the most tragic and disastrous events can have a silver lining.

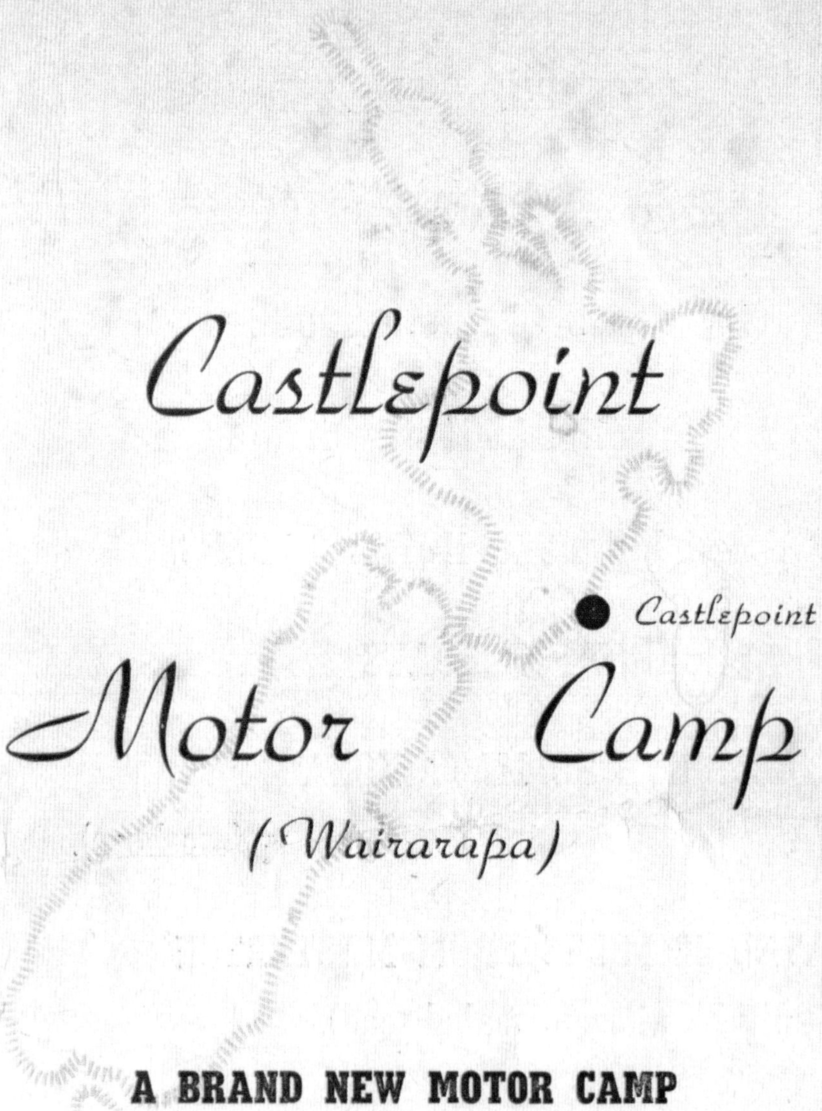

Castlepoint

Motor Camp

Castlepoint

(Wairarapa)

A BRAND NEW MOTOR CAMP

OPENING THIS CHRISTMAS

1968

IDEAL AREA FOR CHILDREN

MOST BOOKS ABOUT ICONIC STATIONS don't have chapters about holiday parks, as the two things are usually mutually exclusive — the serious business of farming and the not-so-serious business of getting away from it all and taking a break in the sun, the sea and the surf don't usually have much in common.

Since as far back as the 1920s, they have been intertwined at Castlepoint. The first sale of sections locally was at Ngamatea, on the foreshore. Scattered holiday homes began to appear, and these increased later in the 1950s when the station began to subdivide sea-front sections for sale and development, as the holiday community began to grow and the station needed funds.

By the 1960s, station management made the decision to develop a camping ground, both as a source of additional income and, more importantly, as an asset that could be sold if necessary to pay any future death duties. By that stage, three of the major beneficiaries of the Johnston family trust were elderly, and if two of the three passed away within the same financial year, the combined effect on station finances would be significant.

The original camping ground was established by the county council on land donated by the station in lieu of contributions that would otherwise have been levied to pay for a recreation area. What is now a busy holiday park, with approximately 120 powered camping sites, thirty non-powered sites, three standard cabins, seven kitchen cabins and two motels on one side of Jetty Road, and five motel units, two flats and three large-group accommodation units — sleeping between them at least another eighty people — on the other, began life as a bare paddock with one tap and a long-drop toilet. If you wanted to go camping in those days, you had to be prepared to rough it.

At first, there was no access across the creek beyond where the main office buildings are now located. The area was covered in tree lupins and driftwood, and was known as the infamous Katipo Flats, with the adjacent sand hill a popular playground for children on holiday. John Sutherland, who now lives in Auckland, remembers playing there as a child; his parents had a bach at Castlepoint, a house his father built, up on the hill. 'We used to spend ages getting up to the top of the sand hills, all for a few crazy moments of hurtling down on whatever we had that day as a slide — and then having to spend ages slogging our way back up again to do it all over again.' He remembers the settlement as an amazing place for a child in the 'fifties, with other attractions being fishing for the huge eels in the creek and, best of all, the chance to help the station-hands by rolling their cigarettes for them when their hands were dirty.

When the holiday park came along a bit later, in the 'sixties, those station-hands had their hands full with its construction. In the 'let's get on with it' way

Previous page: An unadulterated view from the Castlepoint camping ground, developed by the station management in the 1960s.

Opposite page: The first Castlepoint Motor Camp brochure, 1968. *Laing family collection*

that was much more common back then, the station and the council agreed to a land swap, returning the original camping area to the station, which would then use it to develop a modern caravan park and camping ground. At the time, the council was realigning the road between Castlepoint and Masterton; not only would this improve access for cars towing caravans, but it also meant the council had thousands of cubic metres of clay on its hands. This became the basis for the construction of three huge, terraced levels that now define the main camping ground. At the same time water tanks were put in, along with access roads, an ablution block, an office building and, most importantly, a sustained planting programme which saw sheltering macrocarpas put in place.

Right: An aerial view of Castlepoint Station homestead and other buildings to the left of the road, with holiday baches and the newly levelled terraces of the campground to the right.
Laing family collection

Opposite page: The view across the bay from the terraces.
Laing family collection

The sandy, katipo-infested flat below, now housing the main office site and the colourful children's playground, was covered by two feet (60 centimetres) of solid clay; despite delays caused by — of course — the wind, culverts and underground piping and cabling were concreted in place, creating a building site out of what had been a wilderness area. Peter Laing, who supervised the work, recalled: 'One of the biggest problems we faced — once the myriad of drains were dug and exposed — was the Castlepoint wind. We struck an extremely windy spring and the gale nor'westers were just relentless, with sand blowing everywhere.'

As anyone who has ever built anything anywhere requiring building permits knows, building inspectors don't exist to make life easy, and the one with

Castlepoint in his sights at the time wouldn't allow the drains to be filled in until every single one had been smoke-tested.

'It was absolutely brutal trying to work in gale-force conditions, made worse by the fact that these drains were on the nor'west side of the ablution block, totally exposed to the full fury of the winds.' And those northwest winds fair screamed down the valley. On windy nights, so local legend goes, the sound of tent pegs being hammered back into the ground was pretty much continuous. Putting the roof on the ablution block was a builder's nightmare, with Peter Laing describing how anyone who even picked up a piece of six-by-two was virtually airborne, 'like a helicopter'.

In case you're thinking by now that Castlepoint is the only place around here with wind problems, there's an historical footnote to the park's construction to help put it in perspective. The infamous *Wahine* storm of April 1968 — the one which caused the sinking of the ferry *Wahine* in Wellington Harbour — ripped through the whole of the Wairarapa and, among all the other damage it caused, the wind picked up stacks of timber in a Masterton timber yard, throwing it around like matchsticks. Much of it was native timber, and much of it was damaged. Made available at a reduced price as storm-damaged stock, it became two four-berth units up on the second level of the holiday park, with the rest used for more sheds and outbuildings over at the station. Waste not, want not — as true then as it is now.

When the camping ground first opened for business in 1968, it had sixty-eight caravan powered sites and twelve cabins, and was set to become a part of the summer holiday memories of generations of Kiwi children. In those days no one had time to mow the grass, so the station shepherds used to periodically bring in a mob of sheep and erect an electric fence. Over time the 'camping ground' sheep became very docile and used to people. In order to easily identify these 'trained sheep' from the rest of the stock, someone had the bright idea of using all black sheep, and in time the flock became a real attraction for holiday-makers, especially the children.

Nowadays the early station origins of the holiday park are commemorated in the names of the facilities on the landward side of Jetty Road, where the Ranchhouse (the original shearers' quarters), Bunkhouse and Cookhouse now provide sleeping quarters for visitors, including school parties — a long-established Castlepoint tradition. And in case anyone wonders, what they now rent out as the 'Garden Cottage' used to be the old gardener's quarters, in the glory days when the station employed a full-time gardener and produced almost all of its own food.

Managers Kerry and Lynell Ellis came to Castlepoint with their three young children and a caravan more than twenty-six years ago. Since then they've owned and operated the hotel at Whakataki for many years, before a stint operating a holiday park in Whakatane. But, with six grandchildren in the local region, when the opportunity came to move back to Castlepoint as permanent residents they leapt at it.

'As soon as we got here it was like *Oh, God, I'm home*' for Lynell, who has married into the history of the place — Kerry's granddad used to drive a bullock team at the station, and his grandmother arrived at Castlepoint by boat, long before the road was built.

In 2010 the holiday park saw 14,800 visitors, and in January 2011 they had 4500 visitors; the majority are domestic, with most of them coming from Wellington, two and a half hours away. 'It's still very much a family sort of place. We get lots of young ones who come here for the surfing, but it's mostly families. Of that 14,800 we had last year, only 1600 were from overseas.'

Kerry and Lynell run the camp with the help of two part-timers, Jenny Pocock and her husband Kevin, who is also a deckhand for one of the five commercial crayfishing boats operating out of the settlement. They are part of the permanent population of sixteen left at Castlepoint when all the holiday-makers return home.

One of the biggest changes Kerry and Lynell have seen is the impact on the business of the Internet. The holiday park website is now the primary point of contact for most bookings. One thing that hasn't changed is *why* the campers keep coming — the diving and surfing are both superb, and the crayfish and paua still taste just as good. 'People still come here for the fishing. If you've got a boat, then you can catch groper, gurnard, kahawai and even the odd tuna.' You can also fish off the reef, the deepest land-based fishing in New Zealand.

Another thing that hasn't changed is having to educate campers about water shortages — the instigation of a five-minute shower for 50 cents has been more about cutting down the length of showers than about raising revenue. There's no town supply out here, with the camp drawing its needs from springs on the station, which is then stored in the big water tanks. Water tankers bringing water to baches are a common sight on the road during summer, and the issue Peter Laing first identified when the camp opened in 1968 — of 'convincing the campers that a rural water supply was not akin to a town supply' — is one they know all about at the Castlepoint Holiday Park.

From practically everywhere on the station, on a clear day the view is always superb — that's a given — but it's especially true from Cabin Nine which, not surprisingly, is one of the park's most popular. Walking up to the site you might wonder why; there's absolutely nothing there but a small, wooden box-like cabin surrounded by gravel. At first glance it's nothing special, with no grass or garden — the wind sees to that — and instead there are seagulls nestled in the stones, hunkering down against the wind. When you turn around and see the view it all clicks into place. There's not much in the little cabin, which is clean and tidy and basic — just a double bed, a tiny stove, a microwave and a triangular Formica table butting up to the window, but in a spare and economical way that seems perfect when you realize that most of the wall on the seaward side *is* window. Out of that window is a stunning view of the lighthouse and its headland, the sweeping beach where the famous Castlepoint beach race meeting is held, and as much sea and sky as a pair of eyes can drink in. The great, blue expanse of sea and sky just goes on forever, and is utterly, breathtakingly perfect on a perfect day. It's also rather impressive during a big storm.

There's a spare beauty about the place — it's not about gardens and flowers and frills, owing to the ever-present wind, but it's a place to lose the cobwebs and sort out the wheat from the chaff. If you've got a tent, though, make sure it's a strong one.

A traveller's van rewarded by a beautiful dawn after
the long drive in from the Wairarapa valley.

Caravans on the road in to Castlepoint near
the Whakataki Hotel.

The Castlepoint Beach Races

A matter of great local concern every year, around the beginning of March, is the state of the beach. Locals start checking it every day, and commenting on the size and number of exposed rocks. If you don't know why, it can all appear a bit mysterious, but if you know about the famous Castlepoint beach race meeting, and the Castlepoint Cup, then it all becomes clear.

This has been a much-loved local tradition for more than 130 years, a race meeting held at the end of summer, where the horses race along the beach. There's also another race going on at the same time, against the incoming tide — to get through the race card before the track disappears under the water. The horses love it, the trainers love it, and the public love it. It started out as a shepherds' race, with a bottle of rum as the prize, but no alcohol has been awarded for a long time now, and a family atmosphere prevails.

Thomas Guthrie was a keen sportsman, and encouraged the young settlers to develop sporting rivalries with other districts. The wide hard stretches of sand at Castlepoint beach provided an ideal venue. Initially, sports meetings on the beach featured running, jumping, shot-put, hammer throwing, shooting and beach cricket, with a dance in the evening. Guthrie encouraged the station staff to race their stockhorses, which eventually led to the now-famous Castlepoint Cup on race day. The first recorded race was back in 1873 on Boxing Day, and the early settlers and their farm-hands from all along the coast would race against each other for a bottle of rum. It became an annual event, interrupted only by the wars, the Great Depression, the polio outbreak in the 'fifties and those times when unseasonal easterly storms stripped the sand off the beach.

Spectators from Wellington and Hawke's Bay flocked to Castlepoint for the race meetings, which grew in popularity. While it's a family-friendly event now, that wasn't always the case; meetings in the 1890s were characterized by the presence of hustlers, illicit gamblers and fisticuffs on the beach. The women were pretty tough too, by all accounts, with one said to have had a baby in the morning and played an accordion at the dance that night.

Up until 1900, a mile and a half hurdle race was run, using wire barriers, but this was discontinued after a jockey was tragically killed during a practice race. In those early days station staff and Castlepoint residents were the usual winners, with the starting gate a piece of rubber tubing attached to a fishing line and the judges at the finish standing on the back of a truck, sighting against a peg in the sand.

Opposite page:
Scenes from the famous annual beach races, a much-loved tradition for more than 130 years.
Suzanne Wood

The rocks on the beach haven't been kind to the races recently, and it's been six years since the last race, with the 2011 race again having to be cancelled. You have to have a minimum width of ten horses to run safely up the beach, and you also have to find a time when the afternoon tides are right so that the beach will be as wide and as firm as possible in mid afternoon in March, to give you the maximum time for the racing.

In all respects a regular race meeting, there are two special races — the first race of the day is always the Shepherds' Hack, open to bona fide station horses, and the final race of the day is the Stewards' Race, which the thirty-five stewards, and their relations, are allowed to enter. Sarah Crofoot has raced once, and her mother describes the thunder of hooves as the horses run along the beach as truly amazing. Coming from an area in America where rural traditions were increasingly under threat, the beach racing was one that the Crofoots were keen to see continue.

The first race meeting after World War II. *Crump family collection*

Opposite page: Crowds line the foreshore and queue for the equalisator tote. *Suzanne Wood*

Castlepoint Station has always been integral to the running of the races, and the various buildings including the payout tote, bright yellow and blue, are still stored there. Back in his day, Peter Laing could cast his eyes over the number of cars parked in the Quarters Paddock and know whether the meeting was going to be a good one. The annual race meeting was a focal point of the station's year.

Before World War II the betting was run by on-course bookies, but in the 1950s the Castlepoint Racing Club became the first in the country to take advantage of the 1949 Gaming Act, and equalisator betting was introduced. This is rather like a lottery: you don't get to pick your horse, instead you buy a ticket for (say) $2 which entitles you to a share of the winnings if the horse drawn against that ticket wins. There's no payout for second or third — it's winners only, to keep things simple.

Back in the 'forties and 'fifties as many as eighty horses would race, and the station woolshed had to be scrubbed out to accommodate them. Before the roads were improved, Castlepoint was a good half day's drive from surrounding districts, and owners would often bring their horses over the hill to spend a few days there ahead of the race. Some were sleek-looking racehorses, while others were station

hacks that raced under names such as Strewth and Cripes, and were as scruffy as they came. Strewth and Cripes belonged to a local character, John Morrison, who also acted as the race commentator. He used to climb up a ladder onto his platform and use a pair of binoculars to call the races. He mostly got it right. Peter Laing was always amused at the way the names Strewth and Cripes were interchangeable from year to year, although the unprepossessing-looking animals could certainly run.

Horses dumping jockeys and losing saddles were commonplace, and there are stories about animals careering off into the crowd, narrowly missing babies in prams, with others having to be run into the surf to calm them down, and until they started parking the fishing boats across the end of the beach, forays onto the road were common.

In those days the station hacks were extremely fit and fast. One that made a name for himself was Fella, who started in four races one year, won three times and then came second. He was prone to bucking and, according to Peter Laing, you never knew when he was going to let one rip. 'He was a beautiful animal to ride — strong as an ox. The only way he could be stopped along the beach was to turn him into the surf and let him run himself out.'

One of the characters who took part for many years was Freda White. A top horsewoman in her day, she would bring a team of horses with her every year from Feilding. Famous for several things, including an extremely foul mouth and a party trick which involved her standing on her head and drinking an 8-ounce glass of beer (about 250 ml), she was only ever tipped off her horse once. She claimed another jockey flipped her off and she took a hoof to the chest. According to Peter Laing, by the time she arrived back at the woolshed she was 'fair roaring'. She was out to get the so-and-so in no uncertain terms, but first she wanted a bottle of whisky. When told she couldn't drink and ride, she pulled up her shirt, whipped off her bra and said, 'I'm not going to *drink* the bloody stuff.' She wanted it to massage her chest, before making it out to the next race. 'Tough as goat's knees' was Peter Laing's description.

Freda would come down the week before and set up camp, usually with some fair-sized hangers-on who helped to make sure there were no larrikins. 'Nobody ever dared challenge Freda!' On one notable occasion, Freda had broken down en route with her team of horses, and Gordon Meikle was dispatched to Masterton to collect her horses. 'Somebody always came to Freda's aid, and this year it was our turn.' On the way back home, a huge Captain Cooker ran out onto the road and Gordon skittled it. 'The pig was brought back to the woolshed and Jess, a cook from one of the shearing gangs who had come down with Freda that year, turned it into five-star-plus meals for the next couple of days.' Waste not, want not — that's always been the way out here.

In the late 'fifties, dances were held in the woolshed after the races. One of the social highlights of the year, they became a fundraising opportunity for the newly established playcentre, with the mums preparing a good old country supper up at the shepherds' quarters.

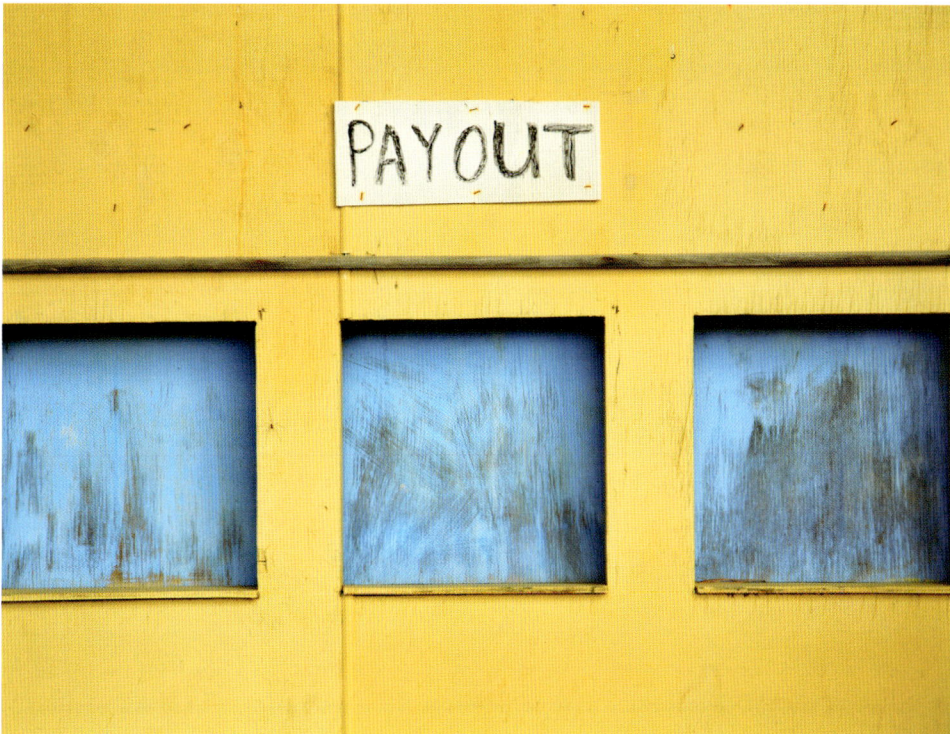

The famous yellow and blue payout tote, stored at Castlepoint Station until race day each year.

When they were running some of the early dances they needed more efficient lighting than the candles and lanterns that were in use at the time, so Freddie Maunsell from Rahui, up Tinui Valley Road, offered his services as an amateur electrician. The only trouble with that was Freddie was colour-blind, and every time they turned the motor on there'd be a bit of a fizz. It took a few lengths of electrical cable before they got things sorted — with the blue wires connecting to the blue wires, and the green ones connecting to the green — and Freddie managed to get the lights up and running.

Freddie's wife, Ray, was a great horsewoman, and in recognition of her dedication to the club, she was made an honorary life member. Their son Bill, also a rider of some renown, is a long-time steward and ex-president of the Castlepoint Racing Club. Keeping it in the family; something they do well here at Castlepoint.

Technology at Castlepoint

Cometh the time, cometh the man. Anders Crofoot has proved the truth of the old adage, as his skills and experience have brought Castlepoint Station into the twenty-first century. Able to adapt the best of the technological aids, he has brought the station to the point where it is now in a position to make the most of the benefits offered by the digital age.

Previous page:
Anders Crofoot
surveys the
landscape on
a clear day from
the back end of
the station, once
an area covered
with scrub.

WHEN YOU'RE DIRECTLY INVOLVED WITH WORKING THE LAND, you are much more aware of the rhythm of the natural cycles which are going on around you. In an office, or living in town, you're less likely to notice the patterns and you certainly don't notice the weather as much; but it's more than that, and goes much deeper. Farmers need to be able to link in to the heartbeat of the land, and know its moods, its composition, its multitude of environmental factors and its long-term cycles. While much of that knowledge comes from working on a property for generations, increasingly farmers are turning to the number-crunching power of technology to help them accumulate and analyse the huge amounts of information and data their land and their stock provide, seeing in that information the ability to improve, enhance and refine their productivity — and their profitability.

Anders Crofoot's particular combination of technical computing skills arrived at a time when the computerization of New Zealand agriculture was all set to happen, and it's certainly accelerating right now, with a lot of things coming together.

The best thing about living at Castlepoint for Anders is the real challenge he feels every day. 'Probably one of the things that gets us out of bed in the morning is that our work here is incredibly complex. Farming requires a huge skill-set in a whole variety of things. For better or worse, you never do the same thing twice. Just because you've solved something once, doesn't mean that the next time it comes around there won't be a little twist to keep you on your toes.'

One of the first things Anders wanted to do when he arrived at Castlepoint was to use his computer skills to keep track of individual paddock performance. 'I'd figured that one of the best things to do was start tracking how many ewes we were set-stocking in each paddock and the lambing percentage for each.' For those of you who aren't farmers, set-stocking is the ratio of ewes to paddock area that's set just prior to lambing; once it's in place you basically leave it alone, to avoid any further disruption to the stock at such a critical time.

'We took our previously recorded area and ran everything through a spreadsheet and started putting the appropriate number of ewes in each paddock, but within two weeks we were shuffling ewes in and out again. Either we'd got our stocking rate wrong, which I didn't think was all that likely, or our paddock sizes were wrong.'

When he looked further into the issue, Anders soon discovered the source of the problem. 'At the time, we had some very nice maps which they'd been using here for ages. However, these were ones that had been prepared by the Catchment Board, who had been mapping basins and water flows; and to be helpful to farmers, they'd drawn in fence lines.' Although it was a 'best guess', the end result was that the maps the regional council had weren't particularly accurate concerning paddock areas.

Fortunately, Anders had a background in geographical information systems and had been involved in a project mapping a watershed in the States. 'When we first came here, I thought it would be really nice to put the whole farm onto a GIS [Geographic Information System], but it's a reasonably expensive undertaking. There was a mapping programme being developed in Masterton so I got a copy of that and tried a few things, but eventually I realized that the paddock areas we had weren't accurate enough for what I had in mind.' All in good time.

A conveyor used to move sheep in a continuous flow for tasks such as drenching and vaccinating.
Ginny Neal

The Crofoots' approach to running the station meant that good tele-communications were essential, and in this they were fortunate: Telecom had started rolling out new technology from Masterton, so that by the time it reached Castlepoint 'there was more modern and better stuff than when they started'. Conversely, at Otahome, where the farm manager and the shepherds live, radio set technology, which is about fifty years old and for which Telecom had never been able to find a replacement, was in use.

'We wanted to do more things on the computer and it became increasingly difficult, and five years ago, when we were looking at how we could handle it, a Masterton ISP, WIZwireless, was rolling out a modern radio data network and we're now part of their system. We have a tower up near Castle Rock, and our internal computer network goes from the holiday park ten kilometres south to

Otahome. This also allows us to spread a wireless signal, so what we're looking at is eventually if we need communications through the cattle yards and things like that it's quite easy to implement.'

For quite some time the station has been using technology to help with sheep weighing and drafting, using Racewell sheep-handling gear. 'It's a neat piece of technology developed by Robin Fagan in Te Kuiti. The sheep come into the confined area, and walk up past electronic eyes, into a crate, which has one side as a moveable wall. As the sheep come in, the wall moves pneumatically and clamps them so that they are immobilized. We basically use it to weigh them, but you can drench them or do whatever else you need to do, and the whole thing has another pneumatic ramp which will lift it all up so that if you want to dag sheep, you don't have to bend over each time. Off the front of the unit, there's a three-way drafting gate, also pneumatically controlled, so depending on the weight range you've programmed in, it sorts the sheep for you automatically.'

The Castlepoint team has been pleased with the performance, finding that it not only does the job more quickly, but it also does it more accurately, making fewer mistakes than human operators. This is hardly surprising, as it doesn't have to bother about a sore back or adverse weather conditions.

Another innovation was a hydraulic petrol-powered sheep conveyor, which saves a lot of wear and tear on those having to manhandle the animals; when you've got 27,000 animals to handle, several times a year, that's worth its weight in gold. The station also uses a Hecton sheep-handler for dagging and crutching, which is basically two dagging units, which can be tipped up to bring the sheep to you. These are located side by side on a trailer that can be taken to the sheep. Anders Crofoot describes it: 'As the sheep come in they're grabbed. You push a foot pedal and it picks them up and you can crutch them. It's great technology, and lots of the contractors are using them.'

One of the advantages is when it's raining and the sheep are wet and full. Traditionally, you'd have to bring the sheep in off the paddocks and allow time for them to dry off and empty out, whereas with the Hecton that's no longer an issue.

'It's a lot easier on the stock: they can be run off the paddock, through the gear and back into the paddock. In this way the sheep are only off-pasture for a couple of hours as opposed to a full day. And it's much easier on the guys' backs.'

OSH would like that.

With a lot of balls to keep in the air at any one time, the farm manager, Stu Neal, says the use of modern technology at Castlepoint was one of the many attractions that enticed him away from the South Island.

'Emily and Anders are so up to date with technology and really pushing the boundaries in that respect, and I've got everything possible available to me as a manager. Anders has systems set up for recording, benchmarking and weighing, and with the sheep-handling systems we have in place everything here to help us achieve the best outcome.'

It's a point that's also made by Rob Kilgour and the other shepherds, who all cite the station's advanced approach to new technology and the opportunity to work with it as one of the attractions of their job.

Stu flips out an iPhone: 'This isn't just for the phone, it's got a wee attachment called iFarmer and all our stock records are going into here. I can have this in the field with me and everything I need to know, or want anybody in this business to know, can go into here and be transferred onto the station database.

'Going home each night and making myself put all the information into a computer is quite a hard discipline, but with this iPhone, hopefully it's going to make all that information much more accessible for everyone in the business. I can do it all where I am, in the paddock.'

Like the rest of the staff, Stu Neal is enthusiastic about the benefits of technology for farming in the future, and the way it's being embraced at Castlepoint. 'The industry is in the process of introducing electronic tag identification for sheep and cattle, with it becoming compulsory for cattle in November 2012. We'll have a wand reader so we can just swipe a microchip off the cattlebeast's ear tag, just like you do at the supermarket checkout — and that can be totally traceable back to our farm. We can send the animal straight off to the meatworks or whatever with all that information about it programmed into its ear tag, whereas at the moment it all relies on paperwork.'

Electronic tagging is certainly one of the developments Emily is looking forward to, along with the associated opportunities it will provide in terms of tracking stock, growth rates, and the response to management decisions. 'We'll be able to align with finishers in terms of taking stock right through and being given hard numbers to use in our selection process.'

One day you'll be able to sit down at a restaurant on the other side of the world, and know that the meat you're eating came from Castlepoint Station, and the on-screen menu will also be able to show you pictures of Castlepoint Station. According to John Tavendale, it's something that's already happening in the United States, where our carpets are being sold. 'They can put the New Zealand story on the screen for you and say these carpets came from this property.'

We've certainly come a long way from that piece of number eight fencing wire.

Farm manager Stu Neal's six-year-old New Zealand
huntaway, a working dog used to push sheep or cattle
away using a deep and piercing bark.

The Castlepoint Horses

Once, the station had more than eighty working horses — now there are thirteen on the property. Back in the day, as they say here, the stables on the property were used extensively; and were a hive of activity day and night. As Sarah Crofoot explains, 'In those days the horses were out working all day, every day, and they didn't have much time for grazing, so they were hand fed twice a day.'

While that doesn't happen any more, before he died former manager Peter passed on some of his knowledge of shoeing horses to Anders Crofoot. The farrier's tools at the station were dusted off and a long-standing tradition continued. In the 'fifties and 'sixties, the number of cattle and the distances shepherds had to drive mobs necessitated the use of horses. Today, when the boys are working with the sheep, quad bikes are used for transport. However, there's been a deliberate decision taken to work cattle with horses.

Stu Neal says that when he first came to Castlepoint and they were working the cattle, the animals weren't intimidated by the dogs and would charge at them, but shepherds on horseback are higher and more naturally dominant — and with Stu, head shepherd Rob Kilgour and shepherd Jared Roberts all riding their own or station horses to work them, he's noticed a change in attitude: the cattle are now easier to work and more respectful of the dogs. The vet bills are lower as well, and for men who love their dogs, that's an important consideration.

Rob has two stockhorses, as well as a young one that he is training. He uses them to work the cattle, where they come into their own. This is especially the case at bull changeover. 'We switch the combination of bulls with the cows every twenty-one days just in case the first one isn't doing the job. It's a lot easier on a horse, and takes the pressure off the dogs because on a horse you can get right in amongst them and give them a bit of a sort out.'

Just like dogs, horses that work with cattle begin their training when they're young. As Rob describes it, 'That's when a rider can teach them what they want them to do, then the horse is much better in any stock-handling situations that arise later.' Not all horses are happy around stock, and Rob describes the problems of horses that have 'come off the track': 'They see cattle and they just want to race them.'

Sarah Crofoot has grown up riding horses, following in the footsteps of her mother. Today, Emily has a driving pony and a gig, although she doesn't get out in it much these days. Prince, the thirty-eight-year-old superannuitant with no teeth, was the patriarch of the station, but recently passed away; Sarah describes him as 'really special — he was the horse the Laing children learned to ride on. We've

Opposite page:
Head shepherd
Rob Kilgour
mustering on 'Kiwi'.

got Chief coming along; he's going to be three in March and was born on the station. I have my pony, Ruby, and my horse, Jordy, both of whom I have ridden competitively (jumping, dressage, eventing). My pony is still fun and a really good stockhorse, so the boys can use her if they need to on the hills. We are hoping to put her in foal this spring to Dusty, a neighbour's stallion who is also Chief's sire.'

Down at Otahome, Stu and Ginny Neal also have horses — including a beautiful twenty-five-year-old palomino pony, named Ralph, and two other horses, five-year-old Robbie and eleven-year-old Hairy, whose sire came from the legendary Molesworth Station. The horses there enjoy a paddock on the clifftop, with amazing views. Robbie has started training for stock work, hunting and perhaps some showing, and Hairy (who goes exactly that in winter) is a very safe and sensible hunter Stu has ridden with both the Starborough and Wairarapa Hunt Clubs. With both parents keen riders, their boys are set to carry on the family tradition.

Asked to describe what makes a good stockhorse, Sarah is in no doubt: 'Stockhorses have to be really sure of their feet and good on the hills, and have to be quiet-natured but have enough tank on them that they can go all day and still run up hills chasing cows if they need to. They can't be spooky, because if you've got a horse that spooks at everything it can be a very long day on the hills. Horses that are scared of the wind, bikes, tractors or rattling iron — they're no use here on Castlepoint.'

Head shepherd Rob Kilgour keeping a watchful eye on the herd.

Having the right people

'It's always interesting meeting the new boys and seeing them grow into their roles. I remember one boy came to us straight from school and he was so excited, he turned up still wearing his school uniform, which made me smile, but it's a real family here — we do things together and everyone takes part in the local show days and dog trials. It's just the way we do things around here.'

Ginny Neal

Previous page: A
shepherd and his
dogs after a day's
mustering.

WITH OVER 27,000 STOCK UNITS SPREAD OVER 2952 HECTARES OF LAND, which is a mixture of alluvial flats, ocean terraces and hill country, Castlepoint Station takes some running. All in all, it has 12 kilometres of coastline and it's long and thin, creating its own challenges.

The structure that has been in place since the Crofoots took over is now much less that of a personal fiefdom, as it was in Peter Laing's day, and more that of a team, with a modern management structure that would be familiar to any number of businesses. There's a farm advisory board, composed of a small team of highly skilled farming specialists who provide input into the farm management decisions, but unlike the board of a normal company, they don't have the authority of ownership; instead, the buck stops with Emily and Anders Crofoot.

For most New Zealand farmers, having an advisory board would seem to be a complicated and expensive way to farm, but for Emily and Anders, who recognized that they had things to learn about New Zealand agriculture, employing a board and a manager was simply being sensible about their investment.

As Anders puts it, 'Our feeling is that two heads are always better than one, and it's the price we have to pay for getting up the learning curve. We didn't grow up here and this helps us get there more quickly. We don't use them for day-to-day decisions, so they're not involved on a daily basis; it's more for setting strategic directions.'

Opposite page, top:
Shepherd-general
Alec Magon at the
woolshed.

Bottom: Experienced
general hand Rick
Graham, responsible
for Castlepoint's
large fleet of
station machinery
— including the
Castlepoint fire
engine.

When asked about the role of the advisory board, of which he is a member, Donald Cooper explains how he and John Tavendale are the two farming voices, along with a representative from a farm advisory company. 'And if we need to, we can bring technical experts in any field into it. The good thing about an advisory board is that it's a small core of people with access to a much wider pool of knowledge.'

Not like in Peter Laing's day, when one man was trying to be it all, and which inevitably became self-limiting. 'After all, you can't know everything about everything, and the most dangerous thing is when people know a little bit about everything!' The most important strategic advantage he sees the advisory board as having is 'the ability to know just who you need to drag in to seek the right advice at a particular time. There's a fine line between getting too much advice and not enough.'

All policy decisions are made by the management team, which consists of Emily, Anders, John Tavendale, the farm management consultant, and Stu Neal, the farm manager. There's been a conscious effort to change the culture, over time, away from the autocratic leadership model that had been practised in

the past, and nowadays the catchword is regular communication, with farming policies frequently reviewed and staff encouraged to contribute ideas for open discussion, although there are times when the owners' opinion carries a bit more weight, since they're the ones with the financial stake.

The general stock policy is focused on a high-performing sheep-breeding system complemented with breeding cows and trading cattle, and the business uses intensive management systems on a large scale. There is also a stock-trading component (sheep and cattle, and with 202 hectares of the Wai Ngaio block becoming deer-fenced, there's also potential for weaner deer).

The management team looks at all the issues around stock numbers and flock/herd structures, stock policy and operational plans, which include the key farming activities of breeding programmes, mating and weaning and, because the station primarily runs sheep, also shearing, animal health issues, feed budgeting and planning. Because meeting performance targets is critical to the station's ongoing financial success, accurate record-keeping is crucial and monitoring important, providing the team with accurate and timely information.

The primary tool they currently use for collating farm data is Baker and Associates' PasturePro System, and Stu provides monthly information for PasturePro. While the team is accountable first and foremost to the owners, they also report to the advisory board and, just as in any other business, there needs to be a strong and sustained flow of information, keeping the board informed of progress towards meeting objectives and providing them with the information they need to assist with strategic planning. The management team considers all the hundreds of factors that affect the profitability and sustainability of Castlepoint, from the application of fertilizer, the subdivision of paddocks and water — both retention and distribution, pasture renewal and the general state of the infrastructure — to the laneway, the tracks and the woolshed and stock yards.

The financier's daughter and the computer specialist/financial analyst have learned their lessons well, and their sustained application of strong business principles to a firm farming base is beginning to pay dividends, as they are now beginning to see the long-term results of some of the changes they first began to implement ten years ago.

There are now five permanent staff employed at Castlepoint: a farm manager, head shepherd, experienced shepherd, shepherd/general and experienced general hand. All have detailed job descriptions, and all are expected to buy into the station's mission statement (see Appendix 1). Unlike some mission statements, which become no more than self-serving platitudes, there's a real sense of commitment and belief in what they're doing today at Castlepoint Station that makes you realize they're serious — and it's working for them. In addition, casual and contract staff are employed as required for specific jobs.

The farm manager's job description includes all the facets you would expect — a good team of working dogs, an understanding of the biology of stock, soils and plants and their respective reproduction, growth and health, and experience with large-scale sheep, beef and deer operations with large mob rotations — and some that you mightn't. These days a farm manager needs an aptitude for new technology and for adapting research findings to the farm situation, with computer literacy high on the list — clearly, mental fitness is as important as physical fitness — and the ability to work with and incorporate advice from outside specialists.

Technical stockmanship and expertise are a given, but good communications skills are essential and in the culture the Crofoots have worked hard to implement at Castlepoint, it's vitally important to be able to both lead and work within a team culture as part of an integrated whole-farm approach, and be able to support any opinion with discussion and debate, qualities that come naturally to the Crofoots, and something daughter Sarah now describes as second nature.

The present farm manager, Stu Neal, came to Castlepoint in 2007 with his wife, Ginny, and two young sons — Angus, who's seven, and Jack, who's five — after several years on South Island properties including Richmond Brook, in his native Marlborough, where he was operations manager.

'When Castlepoint came up, at first we thought no, we want to stay in the South Island — we're South Islanders,' Ginny now says, 'but once we'd seen Castlepoint there was no turning back.' Stu loves the diving here, though the South Island connection remains strong. Every summer there's a trip back to Marlborough and a family get-together at Bulwer, in the outer reaches of Pelorus Sound.

The family lives at Otahome, at the other end of the laneway from Castlepoint itself, with the shepherds also living nearby on the Otahome block. Ginny is a primary-school teacher and has recently taken up a position as a principal release teacher at Whareama School, where their two boys attend.

The Neal boys are growing up in a wonderful environment, and Ginny has come to know the southern part of the laneway rather well. 'I've worked out that I drive 12.5 kilometres to meet the school bus which means a 25-kilometre round trip morning and night, so we're covering 50 kilometres a day all up. With five days a week, that's 250 kilometres and with 40 weeks in a school year that's about

10,000 kilometres a year. We leave here at 7.40 a.m. each morning and I get back here at 8.20 a.m. so that's about a forty-minute journey twice a day, but while it sounds like a lot of time when you put it like that, it's a much better option for us than driving all the way or homeschooling.'

While some people would miss not having neighbours close by and a supermarket handy, Ginny loves the relative isolation, although she has been known to host a morning tea for a couple of hundred farm visitors.

The shepherds live nearby and rapidly become part of the family, with her boys knowing their dogs as well as their own, and happily spending hours out playing with them after school, amusing themselves in the way that kids used to before we started wrapping them up in cotton wool. Each of the boys has his own dog, and one of their favourite games is to hitch one of the dogs to an old baby buggy and ride up and down the driveway — the kind of thing kids get up to when they have to use their imaginations and create their own amusement.

'It's always interesting meeting the new boys and seeing them grow into their roles. I remember one boy came to us straight from school and he was so excited, he turned up still wearing his school uniform, which made me smile, but it's a real family here — we do things together and everyone takes part in the local show days and dog trials. It's just the way we do things around here.'

When they moved onto Otahome, Emily organized 'the boys' to come and cut back the encroaching bush and Ginny has created a welcoming mixture of deep-blue scented lavender with burgundy and white roses and 150 natives behind the tennis court. And in case that sounds a bit girly, the boys' playhouse proudly sports a series of antlers from goats they've shot themselves, and young Jack's pride and joy is the ride-on John Deere tractor with the digger blade he got for Christmas.

The head shepherd is Rob Kilgour, who's originally from another Wairarapa farming family and whose parents farm north of Castlepoint. He spent some time pearl-diving off Broome, in Australia, before coming to Castlepoint, and he and partner Aslynn have a little girl called Byrynn. While Rob's own description of his contribution is modest: 'Doing a bit of stock work and taking over for the station manager when he can't be there — nothing too serious,' talk about him to Stu and there's clearly a lot of respect for Rob's qualities.

'Because Castlepoint is so long and so big, it needs someone of Rob's calibre at this end because the manager can't be everywhere at once. Rob and I are on the same wavelength so Rob knows what I want, which is what Emily and Anders want. It's important for me to have Rob as my right-hand man so I can rely on his eyes and ears up here, because it's such a big place that if you have your finger off the button for a week, things can go pear-shaped in a hurry.'

As well as looking after two younger shepherds, Rob needs to have excellent skills as a stockman, and he's also responsible in part for the accuracy of stock tallies, weights and other data collected for monitoring programmes. He is directly involved in the daily stock management, setting up stock rotations, monitoring pasture covers and feeding. While he's provided with a quad bike and a trailer for his dogs, Rob also has two of his own stockhorses on the property. Because he's out regularly with the stock, pest identification is another of his responsibilities, and he has his own team of six to eight working dogs, each able to control a large mob of sheep or cattle.

To assist Rob there's an experienced shepherd, Jared Roberts, who's originally from the Hutt Valley, and a shepherd/general hand, Alec Magon, who comes from the Bay of Islands. Jared completed a two-year sheep and beef course at Taratahi Agricultural Training Centre, and Alec has a diploma in agriculture from Lincoln — with both describing their 'piece of paper' as an important part of getting work on a good farm.

On a crisp autumn morning, the boys are busy at the woolshed, tidying up a mob of 1200 lambs for the contract shearing gang. When asked to comment on the sheep they're dealing with, Jared describes them as flighty, with characteristic short bursts of speed but not renowned for their endurance. 'If they've had enough, they'll actually sit down when you're driving them.'

The station has had a number of breeds over the years, and went through a phase of predominantly Romneys, but that's not a breed known for its fertility. 'Currently, we're working with what you call Romney composites, and they're roughly a quarter each of Romney, Perendale, Finn and Texel.'

The shepherds all have their own dogs, which come with them to their employment, and they're fed a high-protein, high-energy diet, provided by the station. They burn through a lot of calories during a typical working day. 'That's why we give them fat sheep and high-quality biscuits. They put in a lot more physical work than we do really, so feeding them on skinny, bony sheep is no good.' The same goes for the shepherds, who each receives half a cattlebeast and plenty of mutton from the station each year, although these days they have to do their own cooking. Both boys are provided with a quad bike, and share furnished accommodation at Otahome, in the shepherds' quarters.

Jared usually has five or six dogs, and Alec has two to three dogs. They agree that the dogs are a big part of the attraction of the job for them, with Jared

adamant that he wouldn't be doing the job if he couldn't work with dogs. 'We've seen people try to get sheep into yards without dogs, with rattles and whistles and people running around. Instead of the sheep going in the first time, they run round and go in about twenty times later. At least with a dog, if the dog's good you'll get the job done once so it's the quickest way.'

The shepherds like to get their dogs as pups between six and twelve weeks old and aim to turn them over before they're seven or eight years old to make room for young dogs coming up, although an average working life is up to age ten.

For Alec, being the shepherd/general means that seventy per cent of his time is allocated to stock work and the rest to general work around the station — which can be anything from farm maintenance to fencing, mowing, spraying, shifting breaks, feeding out, and assisting the more senior general hand.

Stock work these days is predominantly yard work — drenching, vaccinating, administering other animal-health products, penning up for scanning, shearing, weaning and conveyor work, and working on the Hecton sheep-handler for dagging. It's not like the old days when shepherds spent long hours in the saddle — and for that they can thank the laneway and the re-siting of the woolshed to a location that's much more central to the property, greatly reducing the time spent moving mobs from one part of the station to another. When the wind is blowing at Castlepoint, that can mean the difference between a good day and a hard day.

Their typical working day generally starts around seven in the morning or earlier in summer. 'It's usually half past five by the time you've fed your dogs and walked in the door.' November and December are their busiest times. 'Then we start about 5.30 a.m. and finish around 6 p.m.'

The other full-time staff member is Rick Graham, the experienced general hand, and he's a very busy man, maintaining the physical structures and operating the station machinery, which includes a Hino truck, two tractors, quad bikes, several Yamaha Rhinos, a bulldozer and a spray rig, so an HT (Class 4) driving licence comes in handy. He also has to keep an eye on the fencing, and because many of the fences on the station are reaching the end of their expected forty-year life span, there's a lot of work right now assisting fencing contractors and installing some major new fence lines.

That he's a pretty useful sort of bloke comes with the territory — especially when you learn that he also has to drive the Castlepoint fire engine, be able to use an arc and a MIG welder as well as a gas plant, keep all the water and pumping systems going, help out with stock work during the busy times, and kill and cut up mutton and dog tucker for the station.

Opposite page: Jill Maunsell, garden designer and caretaker at Castlepoint — no small role on a windy summer-dry station.

Growing the grass, feeding the stock

'There was one year we drilled Italian rye up on the hill here and it simply did not strike, it was so dry. So late winter, early spring, when there was a bit of moisture around we came back and redrilled, and it still didn't grow. We went into a dry spell and it never grew ... then we got some rain in the autumn and off it took. What was happening was that anything that was coming up, the wind was just stripping it off. Fortunately, enough stayed there to take off when it got the moisture. But it was a real example of what happens when you break the rules here at Castlepoint — you pay the price.'

John Tavendale

Previous page:
A rapidly drying
Castlepoint Station
in summer. Prone
to drought, the
land presents an
annual threat to
management and
advisors.

ASK JOHN TAVENDALE WHAT IS THE SINGLE MOST IMPORTANT THING to improve our national pasture, and he's in no doubt. 'Topdressing. That's what transformed hill country in New Zealand, when they started being able to topdress with aeroplanes, because clearing the land now had a purpose — they could do something with it.'

John's a farm advisor, and a former director of Landcorp. While he runs an intensive horticultural business in Ashburton, growing blackcurrants, he's also spent many years advising farmers and station-holders the length and breadth of the South Island. As a favour to a friend, he advised Emily and Anders Crofoot when they were first looking at Castlepoint, and he's now a regular visitor and a member of the station's advisory board.

Improving the performance of Castlepoint's relatively small area of cultivable land has been one of his priorities and, along with agronomist Paul Oliver, the station's management team has been testing out different pasture varieties and monitoring their performance. He's keen to check out the stock and the pastures for himself, and tours the property with Stu, Paul, Emily and Anders, walking out into the paddocks, head down, looking closely at the grass and the soil.

Despite all the benefits of modern technology and scientific research in trying out new varieties, they've come up against the great leveller — the wind — and have fallen back on the sowing methods Peter Laing established back in the 'fifties.

As Stu Neal describes it, the wind just strips out the seed if you try using traditional cultivation methods. 'The most successful method we've found is to use direct drilling, which means minimal cultivation. You're basically spraying the old pasture to get rid of what's there and then you're just drilling straight into the dirt, with a tractor-towed drill. With a direct drill, we have cutting discs in front of the coulters, which push the seed down into the ground, and close-wheels behind, which close the gap and press the soil against the seed.'

Opposite page, top:
Alec Magon moving
a mob of ewe
hoggets (one year
old) over a ryegrass
and clover pasture,
perfect for sheep
— fresh and short.

Bottom: Docking
at the windswept
docking yards
overlooking
Castlepoint.
Ginny Neal

Best Wind Stories

GINNY NEAL:

One of the shepherds had a bike blown over, and it pushed him against a fence and he had to call on his radio for help. When he first called he said something like 'Come and get me bike off me', and we thought something was wrong with his bike and he needed a lift. He needed a lift all right — he'd been asking for someone to come and get his bike *off* him. He'd been blown against a fence, quad bike and all, and the wind was so strong he couldn't lift it off by himself.

ANDERS CROFOOT:

We've lost a number of doors and windows out of the tractor …

EMILY CROFOOT:

There's a preference here for old steel docking yards, as opposed to the lighter-weight aluminium alloy ones — which are light, easy to use and drag around and set up, but they're all together and linked with pins and if you get a big long stretch of them and the wind catches them it can take you and the gates completely away. But the old ones are heavy, and they have steel bars with netting on them so the wind can get through them.

STU NEAL:

We use reinforcing mesh like they use on roadworks instead of scrim and even that's dangerous — if you imagine you're holding it, this is at docking time and we're trying to yard ewes and lambs. The lambs have never seen dogs before since they've been born so they can be quite shy, and we have scrim up at the gate and they won't go past it — that's the idea. We've had students working for us — they're not real strong, and they've had this mesh ripped straight out of their hands. If the wind catches it, you're better off just to let it go. Other times we've had to rescue lambs that have been blown against fences and can't get back up again, the wind is so strong.

ROB KILGOUR:

Up on top of Horseshoe, there's a gate up there where I've been able to sit, leaning back into the wind and it's been enough to hold me up, then when I tried to push forward against it I couldn't.

SARAH CROFOOT:

Some days I've gone out riding and it's been great, then I've got to the top of a ridge and the wind has been so strong I've had to lie forward and just hold on to the horse's neck to stay on, as you feel the wind trying to lift you off the horse's back …

GINNY NEAL:

I'd been in town and I rang Stu, who sounded awful. I asked him if he was all right, and he said, 'I am now!' Turns out he'd taken our son Gus out for a ride on the back of the quad bike to look for his pet lamb and the wind had come out of nowhere, picked up the bike and flipped it over end on end. He felt it going and he only just had time to reach behind and throw Gus off, and he held on to him as they watched the bike go sailing over and over. Poor Gus — he was so upset — he lost his cap in the wind ... We were just so grateful we hadn't lost him!

PETE KLAASEN:

I come from the Bay of Plenty where there's hardly a breath of wind, but I never really believed Sarah when she said there's nowhere as windy as Castlepoint, until you get 150 kilometres an hour of wind and you can't stand up in it. Opening a door on days like that — do it wrong and you can lose a door ...

ROB KILGOUR:

Another time a whirlywind came through and blew the lines off the insulators, so they were hanging down across one of the paddocks. I saw two dead cows in the paddock and wondered what's going on there — turns out the cows had walked into the fallen lines and the high voltage had killed them. While that was a freak event, the wind wasn't. It can get pretty strong around here, quite often when we're riding on the hills on our bikes we can feel them moving sideways with the wind.

STU NEAL:

One Friday, late afternoon, I was up on one of the highest parts of the station and I could see a storm front moving up the coast, but I wanted to get the job I was doing finished so I ignored it and carried on. Next minute the sheep and cattle were bolting down the hill, and leaping over the heads of the dogs, which any farmer will tell you means they're pretty spooked. The dogs were flattening themselves as well, and all of a sudden I was hit by a wave of wind that knocked me flat. A cow and a tree were hit by lightning, and it was all I could do to lie spreadeagled on the ground, hanging on to the side of the hill for dear life, head down in the dirt, waiting for it to pass. When I could finally move my head enough to the side to call Anders down at the homestead, he didn't know what I was talking about and I told him it'd be with him shortly. About twenty minutes later it hit the station, while where I was the sun was out again and you wouldn't even know anything had happened.

When the Crofoots took over Castlepoint, some of the best country on the station was growing poor-quality pasture. While Peter Laing and his team had opened up new land, cleared it of gorse and applied plenty of fertilizer, over time and with the pressure of dropping commodity prices and several years of drought, things had been let slip and the flats were growing a lower quality than the hills.

As Tavendale remembers it, 'Straight away we got into an immediate programme of trying to improve the quality of those sandstone pastures, but it's hard work in this environment. There was one year we drilled Italian rye up on the hill here and it simply did not strike, it was so dry. So late winter, early spring, when there was a bit of moisture around, we came back and redrilled, and it still didn't grow. We went into a dry spell and it never grew and I was thinking, *This is two lots of money we've wasted,* then we got some rain in the autumn and off it took. What was happening was that anything that was coming up, the wind was just stripping it off. Fortunately, enough stayed there to take off when it got the moisture. But it was a real example of what happens when you break the rules here at Castlepoint — you pay the price.

'They were what we call run-out pastures, that had all been cultivated in the past but they were down to browntop and very little clover — just hopeless — so we've now got relatively improved pastures in all that country now, and we're about to start for the second time round. In Stu's time we've introduced lucerne, bringing the good Marlborough influence in, and it's done better than the farm consultant thought it would,' he admits, with a twinkle in his eye.

Stu Neal takes up the story at this point. 'While superficially the conditions might look similar to Marlborough, the difference is that at Castlepoint there's a clay pan, and to successfully grow lucerne you've got to shatter the clay pan so it can get its roots established.' In Marlborough and Canterbury lucerne roots can get down into the shingle and, according to Stu, a lucerne plant in those conditions will put its roots over five metres down into the ground looking for water. 'But with the clay pan we have to deal with, that's not going to happen here.'

The clay pan is anything from 45 centimetres to a metre below the surface at Castlepoint, so they use a subsoiler, dragged along behind a tractor, putting its tines down to whatever depth is set. This leaves tracks through the clay pan so the first set of roots can go in and the water can drain away.

Once you've established your crop of lucerne, though, you've also got to be pretty particular about how you manage it, and that's not in the same way you manage a normal grass stand. 'It's got to be rotationally grazed, which means grazed then spelled, because it grows differently to a normal grass — sending up new runners from secondary growth follicles in the base of the plant, rather than

the actual plant growing again. The difficulty on a large-scale property like this is really effectively managing the new pasture. In order to do that you've got to have a big enough area of lucerne. We've got sixty hectares now, which seems like a very small proportion of the whole place but you have to start somewhere. It's a matter of having a big enough area so you can get a thirty- to forty-day rotation going with a reasonable amount of stock, depending on the time of year.'

Unlike some operations that make hay from the lucerne or, in the past, lucerne meal, here it's grazed *in situ*, and the perfume of a paddock of lucerne in full bloom in late summer sunshine has to be experienced to be believed. With plants covered in flowers ranging from pale lavender through to deep purple, with several shades in between, the air is alive with bees and butterflies, and the smell is glorious, rich and heady and utterly unexpected. They've even seen native bees here, which is encouraging given the impact elsewhere of varroa mites.

Aside from looking great and smelling good, lucerne has a high protein level and is rich in nutrients, which makes it perfect for grazing sheep and promoting lamb growth. 'We use it here in spring for ewes and lambs, and in summer we'd normally use it for lambs, particularly any smaller lambs we finish up with.'

While they've been growing lucerne in the South Island for the past 100 years, it's a new development at Castlepoint. According to John Tavendale, 'With the change in seasons and extreme weather patterns we've been experiencing, we're getting really dry drys and people are asking how they can combat this. While some people are latching on to lucerne as the answer, as if it's something new, it's actually been around for a long time and people have been managing it for all that time. Canterbury and Marlborough have been farming on the back of lucerne for ages.'

Lucerne growers first had to deal with blue-green aphids and the *Sitona* weevils, then plant breeders developed a variety able to resist crown rot and as a result 'we've now got good reliable lucerne stands'. John explains that while traditionally lucerne was cut for supplements and feeding-out at a time of year when there is a feed deficit, now the thinking is for farmers to feed it when they've got it in the ground — in other words make money now rather than spending money transferring it and feeding it out.

The addition of lucerne is one of the innovations that have taken place at Castlepoint; another is the trialling of fescue as a store pasture, the idea being to fill a feed gap on the shoulders of the growing season. 'It grows better later in the autumn and again earlier in the spring than your traditional rye grasses, and recovers from droughts faster,' according to Stu Neal. That's a significant factor here, on a summer-dry property. Any pasture here has to have an eye out for

Ewes penned up at the shearing sheds. The windy areas of New Zealand, especially the east coasts of the North and South Islands, are renowned for their clean and white wool.

drought, so the station tends to favour drought-tolerant clovers and is looking at rye and fescue for the same reason.

But there are limits to what can be achieved by pasture development. Of the total land area at Castlepoint (2952 hectares), there's only 260 to 300 hectares of cultivable land, so the possibility of changing the overall pasture species readily is pretty minimal, given that a typical re-grassing cycle is ten years.

Arable land is limited here, and therefore precious. And with the ever-present possibility of devastating summer drought, it's been protected with water-retention ponds, fringed with rushes and ditches, which nestle in the hollows among the drier hills above. When Peter Laing was clearing new paddocks in the 'sixties and 'seventies, he initiated a policy that the station still maintains today — whenever a new paddock was created, a dam was also put in, creating standing water supplies.

'We're only renewing sixty hectares a year and replanting thirty hectares of that in permanent pasture, so it's a long, slow process. There was a strong initial improvement when we started, but now we're in more of a status quo. In reality only ten per cent of our stock units are carried on that sixty hectares, and the rest of the property is traditional lower-producing hill-country species,' according to John Tavendale, 'and you can't really have a big influence. While we've run nitrogen trials, and you can manipulate the growth rates, in essence these are

A rare break for a working dog — poised for the next command.

low-performing hill-country species and we're not going to change that.' What John does agree they can change are grazing programmes and livestock systems. 'So we're actually making the best use of those lower-performing species, with all the higher-performing species on our lower country for our young stock and our finishing cattle.'

For a station like Castlepoint, while the pasture-renewal programme will improve things it will never have a huge impact. Instead, the increases in lamb weights they have achieved to date have come about through better genetics, better nutrition and better grazing systems, and that's where they will continue to come from.

Emily is determined that they make sure they get the best performance out of their best land during their best growing period, and there's a constant reassessment and re-evaluation of what they're doing, to constantly maximize the condition of the stock and make the most out of the good years — because every farmer knows that not all years are good years.

Stu Neal runs a rotational grazing system whereby paddocks will have ewes in to graze, then no stock at all for forty days, aiming for long spelling periods in summer to give the pasture time to recover; then, in winter, he'll go into an even longer rotation. 'But when it comes to lambing, from lambing to weaning we'll set-stock to ewes all over the property, with so many in every paddock and that's it.'

What has been built up in the pastures each year is what you have to work with when it comes to the business end of the cycle — growing as many fat healthy lambs as possible. John Tavendale points out: 'What this means is that we try to manipulate the pasture growth to feed stock at the critical periods for higher productivity, so at this time of the year, in early February, the next six weeks of Stu's management prepares all the ewes for mating. At the point of mating it's absolutely critical he maintains and quietly improves the weight of the sheep for the first three weeks of mating. If he loses weight at that period the lambing percentages will go down, and it doesn't matter how good a job he's done in the rest of the year, if they're hungry at that time of the year he'll lose.'

When you're manipulating your livestock to get the best performance out of them, what happens in late summer/autumn determines what the station's income will be in a year's time, and how many lambs there'll be for sale in December. 'The day he sells last year's lambs is the day he starts to determine how many he's going to have next year — there are no holidays in this business.'

Stu Neal agrees. 'You take your foot off the throttle, you get caught up and overtaken straight away.'

We grow good wool here

'This country produces carpet wool, and we've just come through twenty years where wool has been just a by-product, which only just paid for itself to be shorn, and now it has finally turned the corner again. The east coasts of the North and South Islands are both very windy, and they grow good wool — it's clean, it's white, and it's good carpet wool.'

Donald Cooper

OVER THE YEARS THERE'S BEEN A PARADE OF SHEEP BREEDS through the station, from Guthrie's original merinos to Lincolns and Perendales, and the station is now experimenting with the introduction of new crossbreeds — with some Finn, some Texel and some Romney — and Donald Cooper says they are starting to see the benefits of some of the associated hybrid vigour, especially in terms of better fertility rates. 'So we're getting more lambs from a lesser number of ewes. In his day Peter Laing was running a lot more sheep to achieve the same number of lambs. In those days it was predominantly store lambs and wool for some of these coastal properties. Wool made up to seventy per cent of their income, now it's probably down to thirty per cent, although that's improved in the last eighteen months.

'This country produces carpet wool, and we've just come through twenty years where wool has been just a by-product, which only just paid for itself to be shorn, and now it's finally turned the corner again. The east coasts of the North and South Islands are both very windy, and they grow good wool — it's clean, it's white, and it's good carpet wool.'

Castlepoint Station aims for a fibre length of three to four or three to five inches (7.6 to 10.1 cm and 7.6 to 12.7 cm), and shear twice a year. In the past they've tried every eight months, but there's been a swing away from once-a-year shearing and the long wool it produces. As Donald Cooper points out, although it's more costly to shear twice a year, sometimes it's cost-effective for animal health reasons. 'We first shear our lambs in January, then six months later in August/September, then they're shorn again in February/March and as a two-tooth in December. At this stage, from then on a sheep on the station will be shorn in May and December. These ewe lambs are ones we'll keep for breeding — at weaning time we keep more than what we know we will need.'

On a clear and sunny morning, with the wind unnaturally quiet, Rob Kilgour and Stu Neal are draughting a mob of lambs up at the woolshed, separating the rams from the ewes, which will then be drenched, dipped and vaccinated, with Jared and Alec busy in the shed with the vaccinating gun.

The rams are being weighed and sorted into saleable lines, depending on what weights the buyer wants; typically this might be lambs over 25 kilograms. In addition, they separate out their prime lambs, those over 32 kilos, which will kill out at a minimum carcass weight of 13.5 kilos — the minimum weight the works wants.

At weaning, everything over 32 kilos comes off and goes straight to the works, while the lambs that fall between 25 and 32 kilos are sold to somebody else to be finished off, to get their weight up before selling them to the works. 'Some years, if we've got plenty of feed we might want to keep some finishing lambs ourselves, if we think that we've got the feed to add value to them — other years we'll sell them on. In this year just gone, we were getting paid good money for store lambs so we were selling lambs down to 20 kilos. We also keep any lambs that are underweight at this stage, and fatten them up ourselves before selling them on in April/May.'

According to Stu, the greatest challenges in stock management at Castlepoint are the wind and the fact that they have a high stocking rate in a summer-dry area. 'So we've got to be prepared to act quickly if the conditions turn against us, and that's why we've got a component of trade stock — lambs and finishing cattle, it doesn't matter which, so long as we're prepared to act quickly.'

Mixed-age ewes, ready for the May shear, after which they are kept for breeding replacement ewe lambs.

Rob Kilgour also reckons the weather is his biggest issue, with the new lambs arriving about the same time as the spring winds. From when lambing starts it's full on for the boys, who are straight into docking, weaning, drenching the lambs again, and continually shifting stock around. During this time in the summer they're usually working a ten-hour day. 'Although each day is different — depending on how strong the wind is blowing.'

And even when it's not blowing strongly enough to stop the shepherds going onto the hills, it can still add a couple of hours on to the jobs they have to do, which means things often don't go exactly as planned. 'But that's farming.'

'Last year we had 15 centimetres of rain in January and the pasture just took off, and as soon as your grass gets long and rank there's no goodness in it — you're better off when it's shorter for sheep. That's the primary role of the cattlebeast on a mixed farm, to keep the pastures down for the sheep, and we hold a lot of cattle in anticipation of the grass being long, to chew the grass off so we get the fresh growth for the sheep.'

While shepherds still tally sheep the same way, with one counting as they run past and calling out 'Tally' for every hundred to his mate who's keeping count, here there's a difference — Rob writes the number in a notebook and Stu enters it into iFarmer on his iPhone. These days a shepherd's basic equipment doesn't just include his horse, quad bike or dogs — there's his cellphone, with an RT for backup, along with his sunglasses and some sunblock.

Pete Klaasen is a close friend of Sarah Crofoot's. He has been coming to Castlepoint for some time, and has been working there over the 2010–2011 summer holiday, having just completed his AgriCommerce degree at Lincoln, where he's about to start his Masters; and he's been impressed by what he's seen at the station, especially in terms of sheep handling.

'Back in the day there was only one set of yards, down here at the coast, so all your sheep at the back of the farm had to come here for shearing. While adding a central lane increased efficiency straightaway, the step after that was to ask why they were bringing all their sheep back here to the station for all your yard work, because they were losing about half a kilo of live weight just walking back, and that's a waste of time and money.' Now there are sheep yards on every second major ridge, five in total, and he has seen how much that has improved stock handling.

'When you're lambing, you set the stock at the number of ewes per paddock to suit the grass so they don't eat the grass right down and you leave them there, because if you move them the lambs can become mismothered. The benefit of having yards on every second hilltop is that they're adjacent to these lambing paddocks, so you can bring each mob of ewes into the yards for docking without having to move them all over the station. This means that if a lamb is left behind in a paddock, it's not that long before the ewes are back again and it's all good.'

Pete sees quantifiable benefits from the stock-management practices at Castlepoint, and credits it back to the station being properly set up, with its sheep-handling facilities right where you need them, meaning you don't have to spend a day moving the ewes just so you can dock them. 'That's just a pain.'

He puts it this way: 'The first idea in developing a property in the past has been to smash all the bush and get grass growing, then you fence around that boundary and know you've got your sheep somewhere inside that area. You then start subdividing it up, and inevitably you make some mistakes when you're rolling out your fence lines.'

After all, it takes a while to find out how the land performs and, in particular, what the wind and water conditions are like over time in a specific area. 'But when a fence lasts forty years, and it's not exactly wrong but could be better, then you don't rip it out — you wait forty years and then you fix it. But because Castlepoint is so old, a lot of that trial and error thing has already been worked through.'

That Castlepoint is big enough to justify the use of radios is also a huge bonus when you're handling large mobs of sheep on the hills, and going down the bottom to check if a gate is open when it should be open, or shut when it should be shut, isn't always possible when you're at the back of a mob of 4000 sheep with your dogs. At times like that, someone else on the end of a radio or cellphone is invaluable — because without you and your dogs, the mob of 4000 doesn't stay as one mob for long.

For Pete, 'The big difference is that it's been going for more than 100 years so you've got a history behind it. In that time you've had managers come along and implement farm policy that's either worked or it hasn't worked and it's been improved on. Over time you've got a sense of what works and what doesn't work here, and that means you've got a solid base to work from.'

That hasn't always been the case on some of the other farms he's worked on, which have been quite a different story, for a variety of reasons. 'When places have no history, or are undercapitalized, you can be working with land that's never been in farmland before and you've got no idea where to start, you don't know how

Contract shearer and rousies in full swing at Castlepoint's six-stand shed.

many stock units you can have on it, you don't know what the risk of drought is — and it's really hard trying to farm when you have no idea where the water sources are. I've also seen sheep/beef properties that have been severely undercapitalized, which meant the property was understocked, the pasture cover was way up and you can't manage efficiently like that.'

Pete sees the difference at Castlepoint Station is in how they're increasing profitability by increasing efficiency, and achieving that by making planned, strategic changes, whereas some of the farms he's worked on haven't seemed to have the same sense of direction. 'For example, one place changed his mind on how many breeding ewes he wanted to have twice in one year — we went from 2500 down to 1500 then he decided he needed to have 4000. He's also playing round with finding the right sheep/beef ratio for his property.'

He sees that a key difference at Castlepoint is having a solid base of knowledge to start with, and a base level of profitability, which enables the owners to increase efficiency with fine-tuning. 'That's good to work for, you can concentrate on increasing efficiency, whereas in the other situation there's no point in trying to increase efficiency in pasture-grazing management if you haven't got enough stock to start with. There's no point cleaning a paddock out properly and getting the efficiency right up if you don't have enough stock to do it in the next paddock. That's the big difference I see in managing this place — it's been set up properly from the start.'

Single-prong steel wool bale hook, used to move large wool bales after pressing.

A controlled burn:
an effective
technique used to
clear scrub during
the development
years at Castlepoint.
Laing family collection

Slash, Rip, Crush and Burn — Clearing the Land

One hundred years after the settlers burned their way across the hills, native manuka had reclaimed much of the more challenging country at Castlepoint. The Great Depression and the economic stagnation of two world wars didn't help, and by the time Peter Laing took charge in the 1950s, Castlepoint had a severe gorse problem, with some of its boundaries blurring into what were described at the time as 'ghostlands' — great seas of scrub.

If he wanted to bring previously cleared areas back into production, Laing knew that he had a battle on his hands. For many years the station had employed gangs of Fijian scrubcutters, but they were barely holding their own against the regrowth, and more drastic measures were called for. With 12 kilometres of coastline, the decision was made to use standing burns, and an intense period of sustained cutting and slashing, followed by burn-offs, gave some encouraging results.

In 1963 things began to hot up, and a bulldozer was brought in to break down the scrub. The first one they tried was too light, a Caterpillar D2, and was soon replaced with a much heavier D4 crawler equipped with a set of Hooper super-giant discs. These were monstrously heavy to pull but proved to be nearly indestructible, after they had gone through numerous smaller blades.

With a blade on the easier slopes and a giant gravity-roller for the steeper faces, Gordon Meikle and his D4 became legendary, especially his unerring ability to defy gravity and avoid crashing down cliff faces. He famously described his technique as simply keeping a small pile of dirt in front of his blades at all times — as soon as the pile of dirt dropped away, you stopped. It clearly worked, as Gordon went on to become the station's longest-serving employee.

Gradually they began to make inroads, and over the course of eight years the D4 logged up more than 26,000 hours as they cleared 348 hectares of bush and scrub. In 1978 they started clearing another area of over 400 acres, this time hiring a Morrow D6 to crush and rip the scrub. When that had been done, helicopters dropped Luma Gel every 6 feet (2 metres), in much the same way as they use napalm today in controlled forestry burns. The resulting firestorm was so intense that they cleared the entire 400 acres within an hour.

As well as the scrub clearance, which continued on throughout the 'seventies, gorse was practically eradicated in the same period. At any one time, two station-hands would be out in the hills with gorse guns — attached to a 900-litre tank of herbicide on a tractor by 60-metre hoses. At the height of the gorse battle, they were spraying almost 4500 litres a day.

Another aspect of Castlepoint's stock management that has impressed Pete comes as a function of its size. 'This place is big enough to sustain technology. A lot of people think if you have the technology, you can have the size, but it also works the other way round. You need the size in order to support the cost of the technology, such as the big dagging plant and the sheep real-weight crate and the sheep conveyor — they all make life much easier, but if you don't have the numbers of stock to support that investment it makes it really hard. When you've got bigger stock numbers, then the cost per head for a small farm with only 4000 ewes is relatively much more expensive than if you have 20,000 ewes.

'Here, sheephandling in general is really nice because although you're dealing with big numbers, the technological aids make it really easy, which makes this a good place to work.'

In terms of land area, Castlepoint isn't one of the biggest properties of its type, but its long history and intensive development over a sustained period of time has meant that compared with its total size it has a large number of effective hectares. Another coastal property nearby is at least three times bigger in land area, about 10,000 hectares, while Castlepoint is around 2900 hectares. However, they have a smaller proportion of effective area, so while they're much bigger on paper, Castlepoint has the better stocking rate. A station is anything from 2000 to 30,000 hectares in size, and while Castlepoint is at the lower end of this range, their stock-to-land ratio is relatively high, at seven to eight stock units per hectare.

A lot of brainpower goes into managing stock these days — and while nature has provided a good, healthy environment for growing wool and meat, there's a mountain of work behind every fat lamb, steer or bale of wool that leaves the property. Farmers now have many more tools at their disposal, and much more knowledge about the processes at work than their predecessors, but with that knowledge comes added layers of complexity and many more pieces to the puzzle.

Pete Klaasen describes it this way: 'Take any farm these days — you have thousands and thousands of decisions you have to make: how many stock units, what sort of stock, what breed, are you going to mate them, when are they going to lamb or calve; drenching, vaccinating — which drenches, which vaccines and when, what species are you going to grow in your pastures, what feed crops are you going to grow, are you going to buy in feed, are you going to graze off or sell animals, if so how many, and when is the best time?'

That's the challenge in farm management nowadays — how to identify the optimal set of decisions for a property and its resources. Says Pete, 'Every business has a limit to its resources and you have to decide on the best use for those resources, and the time something takes to do is one of those limited factors —

what's the best use of the time I have available at any given period of the year?'

Farming is now a multi-million-dollar business, and while some decisions are still made on the back of a horse while you're out reviewing stock, that usually comes after a lot of time spent researching options and running models on the computer to make sure it's the best decision.

Wool bales waiting to be loaded. They are marked with the Castlepoint 'G', one of the oldest wool marks in New Zealand.

'These days, if you own a property you spend a fair bit of your day behind a computer and you've got to understand the business side of things — marketing, law, accounting — it's multidisciplinary, and you have to know a heck of lot about all sorts of things now — animal husbandry, pasture management, human resources, accounts, PAYE. Being a farmer isn't about being covered in shit all day.'

It certainly isn't, and it's probably one of the reasons why there are no flies on the people here.

Fresh wool clip prior to pressing.

Managing Castlepoint Station today

The station has come full circle, and has returned to its origins as a family farm. Once again, a family has come from the other side of the world, to make a home for their children on the summer-dry hills beside the restless Pacific Ocean. While some of the stock-handling methods have changed, the rhythms remain the same, and the seasons still roll through the hills. Some are good, some not so good — but the hard work is the same. And when the wind is still and the sky and the sea are blue, it is like no place on earth.

EMILY CROFOOT AUTOMATICALLY THINKS IN ACRES and describes her home as 9500 acres, comprising three blocks which have been annexed over time. The original Castlepoint block, which was what came down from Thomas Guthrie's original 30,000 acres and which Peter Laing had managed in his day, had no access to the south, so in 1995 the management board sold the summer-safe property it held at the time at Mount Bruce and annexed Otahome, the next property to the south.

Since they've been at Castlepoint, the Crofoots have added two major purchases, buying back the motel units to add to the holiday park and picking up Wai Ngaio, a 750-hectare property adjacent to the Otahome block. The Wai Ngaio block had 135 hectares already planted in pines, 200 hectares in native pasture with a very low fertility, and about 400 hectares of scrub, which they thought could also be planted in trees. 'Our feeling is we would much rather have poorer-quality land in trees to balance the livestock emissions on the farm rather than the land that had been carefully developed over time.' The long-running debate over carbon credits and methane emissions has naturally seen a lot of changes in policy, and Emily accepts that it's an evolving process. 'The rules were continually changing, and it's taken two years, but we've finally sold the carbon credits and so we're taking advantage of that opportunity.'

Farming is farming wherever you go, but there were always going to be differences, as well as similarities, between Mount Kisco and Castlepoint.

'The three differences that absolutely stand out for me are the metre of frost on the ground in winter, which means you never run water pipes on the surface, the huge amount of time you had to spend growing and harvesting winter feed and then feeding it out, and the third one is predators. Even though we lived an hour away from the city, we had a real problem with coyotes moving down from Canada, and regularly lost sheep at Braewold to coyotes.'

As a result of her family's close connection with New Zealand, Emily knew it didn't have to be like that. 'As well as lots of Kiwis coming and staying with us and helping out at Braewold over the years, and lots of letter-writing with friends and relations, I'd spent quite a bit of time down here when I was younger and I was continually reminded of how much time, energy and expense we had to put into managing the climate in North America. Whether it was putting up winter feed, putting up loafing sheds for stock, putting in storm windows ... so much of what we had to do every year was climate-related.'

There are still climate issues at Castlepoint — only here it's dealing with wind, erosion and drought. 'Look at the big picture. At Braewold we had to have loafing sheds, or run-in sheds, if the grazing land was any distance from water — basically

Previous page:
A topdressing plane comes in to refuel at the airstrip.

Opposite page:
Always something to work with — Emily Crofoot at home with Holly.

this is an area of shelter where the stock are free to come in and out of the weather, and where they can get food and water. Which in turn meant you had to supply electricity — to get the water there and to stop it from freezing. Once you start to look at the logistics of that and you look at labour unit per stock ratio, all of a sudden you realize Castlepoint is carrying in the vicinity of 27,000 stock units and doesn't regularly produce any winter feed — whereas at Braewold we were producing winter feed for feeding out five months of the year. All of the water here can be run above ground without freezing, while there the pipes would have to be buried in the ground, which also meant providing electricity to stop them freezing in winter. So looking at the bigger-picture issues, Castlepoint has so much in its favour, all of which allows for a much more extensive operation here and a much better ratio of labour unit to stock unit.'

Just the fact that there are no predators is a huge bonus. 'When you look at it that way, you see that the amount of time it takes to put sheep in at night and let them out during the day doesn't relate to product out the gate, except that's what has to be done in that climate.

'So we just kept focused on those big pictures and within that you manage for wind, you manage for erosion, but our feeling is that wherever possible we work with the land, we don't try and fight it. We see the vast spaces as something to work with.'

For Castlepoint nowadays, the income from those 27,000 stock units is about sixty per cent from lamb (either store lamb or prime lamb sales), about twenty per cent from wool and twenty per cent from cattle. This has changed from the years of wool's heyday when the station's income was seventy per cent wool and thirty per cent cattle. 'We used to breed about 15,000 ewes, and we've found that by dropping that number to 13,800 ewes to the ram, we have more flexibility. We still keep the same stock numbers, but we're keeping more lambs. And now we have breeding stock — both sheep and cattle — with their offspring becoming trading stock, which can be sold, partially finished or finished all the way, with the best ones going back into the breeding pool.'

Emily believes that wool is relatively easy to grow in that provided you can keep the sheep alive and fed reasonably well, they do the work for you. 'Wool is probably a higher percentage of our income than most of the farms around here, with a lot of places having shifted from wool to meat production, which is much more difficult because you have to get a lot more things right and grow the animal well.'

In her opinion that's been a major change, and one that rapidly sorted out the really good farmers. 'To produce good meat you have to feed them well and consistently, and in this climate that isn't so easy. Farms with better country can do it better, because they can make and produce better grass. It's been a major change in New Zealand agriculture, especially through the East Coast, where the going is a bit tougher.

'You go into dairy country and dairy has always been dairy, but most of this summer-dry country is best suited to wool production and did that very well through the 'fifties, 'sixties, 'seventies and 'eighties, and then as the price of wool dropped, a lot of those properties struggled.'

Right now the politics of wool marketing are occupying a lot of Emily and Anders' attention, and it's an area in which Emily would like to see wool-growers having a bit more muscle. 'We see there's a great irony — we have a known product the market is clamouring for and we have hill-country land well suited to sheep production both in terms of land use and tourism value, so we have good use of land — the sheep are doing their bit, but the problem is with the people. Over time many people have been deeply committed to wool, and they've put a lot of time and money into many different initiatives, but the way things are now it's so fragmented, overseas customers are confused, and we're weak sellers, bidding against and undercutting each other. While some people have managed to win some good contracts, nobody's got the critical mass to grow demand. We've learned that there's a core of amazing people who want to see wool valued for what it is and see the opportunity for the market to grow, and we see that having wool valued at its true value, which means having a third income stream, is the very thing that's going to keep sheep and beef properties profitable.'

A Tiger Moth topdresser landing at the former airstrip — Castlepoint beach.

Off the Backs of Sheep

Once an area of land had been cleared, burned and sprayed, the next logical step was recultivation, to bring it into production as new pasture. Through his early involvement with the New Zealand Grassland Association and the Department of Scientific and Industrial Research (DSIR), Peter Laing was to become a master at establishing new pasture on recently cleared hill country — something he now had a lot of at Castlepoint. Before too long, the station became a testing site for fertilizer trials.

To prevent gorse regrowth, they would burn the crushed scrub in autumn and then oversow with grass and clover seeds — usually from the air, but occasionally Peter would sprinkle clover seed on the backs of newly shorn ewes before returning them to their paddocks.

Oversowing was then followed by molybdic superphosphate; in their busiest year, Castlepoint applied 660 tonnes of superphosphate and 600 tonnes of lime. It was the era of aerial topdressing when old Tiger Moth, Beaver and Fletcher aircraft used Castlepoint's hard sandy beaches as landing strips. Aerial sowing made all the difference at Castlepoint, as they were finally able to broadcast seed over large areas and fertilize parts of the station otherwise virtually impossible to reach.

The infamous, ever-present wind had made previous attempts at seeding expensive disasters, and it was during this period that Peter Laing developed the direct-drilling process they are still using today at the station, for the more accessible areas, as the most effective way of combating the wind's ability to strip away seed and soil in a very short space of time.

Over time the old planes were replaced, and when the weather was right, helicopters and trampling mobs of sheep were used to bring in new pasture. The results were staggering.

In 1965 Castlepoint Station had increased its effective land area from 1281 hectares to 2189, all of which had been drastically improved by aerial topdressing. Another way of measuring the success of this sustained assault on the ghostlands is to look at the number of stock units on the station. These increased from 12,500 in 1966 to over 20,000 by the end of 1986, with ewes in the same period rising from an average of 45 kilograms with a ninety per cent lambing rate to 55 kilos and 115 per cent. In 1966 the station sold 47,900 kilos of wool — by 1986 this had improved to 110,000 kilos.

No wonder they say Peter Laing left his mark.

Right now there's huge pressure on properties like Castlepoint, which are sheep/beef producers, as profitability falters. In the lowlands that pressure is coming from the dairy industry, and in the poorer hill country from forestry. But as you would expect from someone who has worked so hard to make it here to farm in New Zealand, Emily Crofoot is passionately committed to what they do at Castlepoint, and equally passionate about the future direction of the wool industry in this country.

'We know that what we're doing is a good use of this type of land, and we see the potential of the wool industry as one worth fighting for. We have a market that's rediscovered wool and we're working very hard to encourage growers to amalgamate. While various brands have been developed, we feel very strongly that no one has the growers' best interests at heart more than growers themselves.'

The wool debate is an important one for Castlepoint to be involved with, as the Wairarapa, and the East Coast in general, grows particularly good carpet wool, and with a property as open as this station, they grow wool with good colour and a very low degree of vegetable matter, which are both very desirable features the marketplace is in the process of rediscovering.

'This is one of the advantages of being a summer-dry property — which means that although rainfall here is about 970 millimetres, the bulk of it tends to fall in the winter. We get very little summer rainfall and the hills typically go golden in summer.'

This year has been a good year, with 100 millimetres of rain falling in January, a time when they would expect to get between 30 and 40 millimetres; and as a result, the hills are flushed with green. When a southerly change blows through, dropping the temperature, they're optimistic that the flush will stay.

Typically, the rains start to fall in late summer and autumn, which is the station's most critical rainfall. 'From a stock-management point of view, you want the ewes to be tupped on a rising level of nutrition and building up our ewes for the winter is key.'

Castlepoint Cattle

You could be forgiven for thinking that Castlepoint is all about sheep; while there are certainly a lot of them, there's also a growing herd of breeding cattle sharing the hills.

Castlepoint has come a long way from the days of Peter Laing and his roving mob of Castlepoint grasshoppers, as they were known, infamous for hoovering up every spare bit of grass on the roadside. There used to be a big herd of breeding cows here before, then the station moved away from them and now they're back again — essentially as a breeding operation, where calves are taken through to a certain age and then killed. Donald Cooper describes them as a 'buffer mob', able to be sold on 'if the season goes against us'.

The station now has a small but steadily growing herd of breeding cows composed of Angus and Charolais breeds and Angus–Hereford crosses. Because it's not good country for running bulls, which tend to tear the ground up and fight, the calves are steered here, and the station has returned to a breeding, not finishing, operation.

The cattle are doing well, and Emily has been taking part in a research programme to train the cattle to eat Californian thistle, one of the weeds the station battles against, with some success. On a visit to her brother Steve's ranch in Montana, Emily had seen the results that could be achieved in an expansive rangeland situation, and has been trialling the programme at Castlepoint. Over a ten-day period, the cattle are trained to eat thistles via a controlled feeding programme which involves introducing chopped-up thistles to their feed. The cattle are put into a smallish, but not bare, paddock. There they are first given hard feed, which they like, with other feeds gradually introduced, ending up with the chopped-up thistles which the cattle by then munch happily — with a mutually beneficial result all round when they are reintroduced to the hill country.

'We had come here as a family after I finished high school, and I just fell in love with New Zealand,' says Emily. 'I had always intended to take a gap year after high school and then go to Cornell University. I'd always been a good, diligent student, but at my first lecture at Cornell we were told to look to the left and look to the right because only one of the three of us would be there to graduate and I thought, *That's not going to be me; that's not the way I learn*, and I realized I'd enrolled in a programme in biological sciences that was very much a pre-veterinary-engineering and pre-med weeding-out course. I didn't thrive in that

Castlepoint's Hereford breeding cows. Although cattle numbers are predominantly made up of Angus, the station retains a small number of Herefords. The Herefords are put to an Angus bull to give first-cross calves, which are then bred back to Angus.

environment and after one semester, a good friend was getting married in New Zealand so I came over and stayed for six months, working for room and board. After that trip I applied to Lincoln for a wool-classing course in 1976, but in those days the only way you could attend Lincoln as a foreign student was as part of an exchange programme. I was turned down, and it gave me great pleasure when I did a leadership course, much later, to be able to put in my course bio that it was very nice to be studying at Lincoln after all of these years.'

When they were first enquiring about the property, Anders was rung by the real-estate agent, who asked him if he knew what his wife was doing, and telling him she was making enquiries about buying a property in New Zealand, to which Anders replied, 'Why not? It's her money.' This was probably an interesting snapshot of a cultural difference of the times, when women were not typically found at the head of large-scale farming operations; that's now no longer the case.

'It's taken time but people are used to me now, and I was pretty careful to keep my head down and not offer an opinion until I was asked. I was careful not to put myself out there and I think, in terms of the operation here, where people were very much used to leadership from the front, allowing and encouraging people to express their own potential took a bit of getting used to and was originally seen as a sign of weakness. But now anybody who is involved with this operation knows that's the way we do things and it's non-negotiable.'

Emily's parents, Jim and Twink Wood, are now genuinely delighted to have another home to visit in New Zealand, although this wasn't always the case. 'We waited until Dad made the decision that he wanted to sell Braewold in his lifetime and we respected that decision. Once he'd made it, we said if we're going to fulfil this life-dream of farming in New Zealand, we'd better get on and do it.

'I think it would be fair to say that Dad was very concerned at the time that we'd be getting in over our heads. As it was going to be such a bold move we sought advice from friends in New Zealand and the States who could be independent of the emotional issue. At the time I think that not being consulted hurt Dad, but we knew we needed to discuss this with people without the issue of "my grandchildren are going to be growing up on the other side of the world".

'While our move here was very fast, it wasn't a mid-life crisis. It was a decision that was a lifetime in the making — as a dear friend in the South Island described it, it was like spending twenty-five years building the foundations, then putting on the roof in a fortnight.

'While we had the assets, we weren't liquid at the time we purchased. We weren't worried about it, but when it had all been done, Anders and I travelled to a funeral with my father, which meant we were trapped in the car for three hours either way and, sure enough, out comes the comment that's now gone down in family history: "I cannot believe that I raised a child with such fiscal irresponsibility."

'Fortunately, by the time we were five years down the track history had been reinvented, and to listen to Dad now he's so enthusiastic about the move you'd think it was his idea! Now he and my mother are genuinely happy that we're here and that so much of the old furniture from Braewold lives here too, now that they have moved into a retirement home.'

A year after they moved to Castlepoint, Emily and Anders appeared on a *Country Calendar* programme. At the time, Emily saw huge advantages in New Zealand for people like the Crofoots, who were committed to farming and living in a rural community. 'The infrastructure is much stronger here, both in terms of markets and supplies and resource people ... Agriculture had moved away from our area in the US and services like tractor repairs or somebody to teach us artificial insemination of cattle, all of those things just kept getting farther and farther away, and you just didn't have a pool of skilled agricultural resources to call on. That's been one of the pleasures in being here — being able to go to field days and farm discussion days and to have all that at our fingertips is just wonderful.'

Coming from a family tradition of rural community and service, the Crofoots made a real effort to get involved, and it has seen them play an active part in their children's schools and the church, with Emily playing for Sunday services at both nearby Tinui, where the children went to primary school, and Castlepoint.

'The first Christmas we were here they asked me to play the piano at church and I thought *Yeah, OK* — but when I started to play "Away in the Manger" I wondered why everyone was singing a different tune.' That's when Emily realized that there was an American version and a Kiwi version of the old classic — and they're not the same.

With Anders now the local fire chief, Emily is also on the fundraising committee for the volunteer fire brigade as well as being involved with the annual Castlepoint Fishing Tournament — a combined fundraising effort where seven local organizations get together each January to hold a fishing competition.

Anders is heavily involved with Wairarapa Federated Farmers and the New Zealand Grasslands Association, and Emily is on the committee of the local Ratepayers and Residents Association; as well, the station is part of two different farming discussion groups. While this sounds like a lot, 'It's not any more than back in the States — my family has always done things like that; after all, we know just what it takes to make a community.'

As for the future of Castlepoint Station, she and Anders are very grateful for the strong foundation that exists because of the development work that was done in the past. 'And with the additional infrastructure we've put in place, we're in a very good position to be able to be adaptable going forward.'

The Castlepoint Logo

Throughout this book you will notice the stylized lighthouse logo, circled by the words Castlepoint Station, with two little capital Gs within their own circles. It's the new station logo, and you'll see it on the staff's shirts and their business cards and at the station itself, on signage.

There's a variation for the holiday park, and it's an outward sign of the depth of thinking and planning that has gone into making Castlepoint Station what it is today, as well as an acknowledgement of its historical beginnings and its iconic status, both as a station and as an important part of the seaside community. That's why the lighthouse is there, and the wavy line which recognizes that here there are a lot of hills, and not much flat land. What most people won't realize is that the little Gs stand for Guthrie —the circled G is one of New Zealand's early cattle brands, registered by Thomas Guthrie, Castlepoint Station's founding settler.

The design was a combined effort from the Castlepoint team, with John Tavendale credited with the final touch — balancing the circled Gs on either side.

'I feel very good about where we are right now — things are finally coming together,' Emily says confidently. 'We've worked through a lot of the issues growers have when they set out to build performance and bring their livestock into higher rates of performance; now we're fine tuning rather than having to take major strides.'

And the future — is it going to be about following international models which have seen the wholesale amalgamation of individual farms into large business units?

'I think there'll be a bit of everything — and a lot will depend on individual succession plans. We see the station as an opportunity for our children, not an obligation. Yes, this has been our dream and yes, they are the seventh generation of a farming family, but we don't want this to be a noose around their necks to stop them from doing other things. But there are opportunities here for them, both in terms of tourism and farm production, if that's what they choose to do.'

It's all about choices in the end — and timing. The choices Thomas Guthrie and Emily and Anders Crofoot made are very similar, although they took place in different centuries, and in very different circumstances. Each wanted a better life in a new country for their children — and it seems fitting indeed that, after all that time, all those years in between, once again Castlepoint homestead is a family home, where children are growing up, and grandparents come to stay and knit sweaters and trim the agapanthus down the driveway.

The hills are quiet now; the wind, the ever-present wind, has dropped a little and the fronds on the date palms in the driveway are murmuring gently. The paddocks are stocked with fat sheep and sleek, shiny cattle, behind fences and gates that lock together in every combination known to man — and then some. Emily's dust-covered Rhino is parked beside the garage, and Anders wants to see what the weather forecast is for tomorrow.

The dogs have been fed, and down at Otahome the young boys have done their homework and the shepherds are getting tea and catching up on a bit of television. Stu's boots are out the back door, Ginny's fed the chooks and collected the eggs. The wind is blowing across the hills and the laneway's catching the last of the sun along the clifftops, while down below surf is pounding through the gap, and the lights are coming on at the homestead.

Angus and Angus-cross breeding cows, prior to set-stocking
and calving.

Appendices

Appendix 1

THE CORE VALUES OF THE CASTLEPOINT STATION BUSINESS

- People, animals, the land, machinery, buildings, and tools will be treated with respect.
- There is accountability throughout the business structure, which provides a system of checks and balances. This should not be viewed as threatening. Performance will be the key judge of all our business relationships.
- The process is as important as the end result (the ends do not justify the means).
- Policy decisions must only be made at the management team level.
- Honesty, integrity, and loyalty are important traits for all employees.
- Observations from all employees are welcomed and ideas will 'get to the table' for discussion. Once a decision is made, everyone is expected to get behind and respect the operational decisions.
- The 'team culture' allows everyone to excel in their areas of strength. The strength of the leadership is in allowing this process to happen. As a team, 'we' do things (rather than 'I'). Within the 'team culture' there is a hierarchy which needs to be respected.
- Everyone working here must want to be here, and ideally see it as a privilege to be working on Castlepoint Station.
- As owners, we will endeavour never to 'pull rank' in the field.

THE MISSION STATEMENT

- To establish a premier Wairarapa property, which profitably and sustainably produces quality livestock and their products, as well as provides a range of accommodation.
- To enjoy the Castlepoint business (farming and tourism) by building a team culture.
- To grow the asset in terms of both annual earning ability and capital value.

AGRICULTURAL DIVISION
- To be grass brokers in the most profitable and efficient way, while maintaining the sustainability of the land.
- To achieve a level of performance and returns that is at the leading edge of summer-dry properties.

- To make accessible the information developed on the station to others, through the training of young staff, and participation in research and field days.

Business description

Castlepoint Station is a well-known Wairarapa property. It is situated on the coast, 60 kilometres east of Masterton and comprises 2952 hectares (2794 hectares effective) of land, with alluvial flats, ocean terraces (approximately 300 hectares cultivatable) and hill country; 202 hectares are deer-fenced. In March 2008, an adjoining 830-hectare block, Wai Ngaio, was added to the Station.

The business consists of a farming enterprise as well as a holiday park and motels.

Ginny Neal

Appendix 2

13th century	Kupe lands at Rangiwhakaoma.
16th–18th century	Maori settlement and occupation.
1770	Captain Cook records Castle Rock in his ship's journal.
1839	Founding of the New Zealand Company.
1840	Arrival of Thomas Guthrie and his family on the *Adelaide* at Port Nicholson.
1843	Arrival of Colenso and Williams at Castlepoint.
1846	Native Land Purchase Ordnance made native lease arrangements illegal.
1847	Thomas Guthrie leases 30,000 acres at Castlepoint.
1848	Thomas Guthrie brings his family and flock to Castlepoint.
1850	John Groves arrive at Castlepoint.
1853	Land Commissioner Donald McLean purchases Castlepoint block.
1863	Castle Point Rifle Volunteers formed in response to the Hauhau movement.
1865	Guthrie sells 10,000 acres to the Reverend JC Andrew.
1873	GM Waterhouse purchases Castlepoint. First recorded beach race meeting.
1874	Thomas Guthrie dies and is buried at Castlepoint.
1876	Castlepoint sold to Walter Woods Johnston.
1879	Death of Anne Guthrie at Porangahau.
1907	Cecilia Johnston, widow of Walter Johnston, inherits Castlepoint.
1913	Castle Point Lighthouse established.
1922	Cecilia Johnston dies, leaving Castlepoint to her four daughters.
1928	Ferdinand Ashworth becomes manager of Castlepoint Station.
1942	Wairarapa earthquakes (one magnitude 7.6).
1948	The Ashworths retire, and Stewart Harvey becomes station manager.
1948	Peter Laing begins at Castlepoint as a shepherd.
1949	Castle Rock and Castlepoint are gazetted as place names.

1955	Stewart Harvey retires and Peter Laing becomes manager.
1959	Electricity comes to Castlepoint.
1968	Castlepoint Holiday Park opens.
1977	Castle Point Scenic Reserve gazetted.
1988	Castle Point Lighthouse automated.
1991	Peter and Nan Laing retire and Trevor Smyth becomes manager.
1998	Emily and Anders Crofoot purchase Castlepoint Station.
2002	Crofoot family become New Zealand citizens.

Below: Stu Neal leading the way along the coast to Castlepoint from Owahanga. *John Bougen*

Opposite page: Surf rolls in at the foot of Castle Rock.

A clear, crisp winter morning across Castlepoint Station,
looking south to the forests at Wai Ngaio.

Castle Point Lighthouse after sunset,
contending with a full moon.

'The dock', wet from seaspray, Castlepoint reef.